INSIGHT GUIDES

EXPLORE

KRAKOW

CONTENTS

CATHOLIC VISITORS

Visit John Paul II's student digs (route 7), the site of his first Mass as a newly qualified priest (route 3), and go to Mass yourself at St Mary's Church (route 1).

RECOMMENDED ROUTES FOR...

COURTING COUPLES

Moonlit walks around the Planty (route 11) are what romance is all about, while a kiss by Sigismund's Bell (route 3) is said to guarantee eternal love.

GOURMANDS

Main Market Square (route 1), with its rich variety of restaurants and cafés, is a foodie's dream, while a number of delicatessens on ul. Floriańska stock a wide range of tasty Polish treats to take home.

JEWISH KRAKOW

Kazimierz (route 4) was for centuries Krakow's Jewish heart; the Old Synagogue remains a symbol of the city. Don't forgo the poignant former ghetto around Plac Bohaterów Getta (route 12), or Auschwitz (route 15).

NIGHT OWLS

Main Market Square (route 1) is surrounded on all sides by cafés and bars that stay open late; Kazimierz (route 4) is considered the real home of Krakow nightlife by those in the know, however.

THE RICH AND FAMOUS

Take dinner at Wierzynek (route 1), the city's most expensive and exquisite restaurant, before going on a spending spree in the boutiques of ul. Grodzka (route 7).

SHOPPING

The little stores of Wawel Hill (route 3) and the Cloth Hall in Main Market Square (route 1) offer fine local wares, while the huge Galeria Krakówska (route 11) has all your favourite international brands.

SOMETHING DIFFERENT

Make a beeline for the Socialist Realist enclave of Nowa Huta (route 13), or Poland's oldest salt mine at Wieliczka (route 16).

INTRODUCTION

An introduction to Krakow's geography, customs and culture, plus illuminating background information on cuisine, history and what to do when you're there.

Wawel Castle in deepest winter

EXPLORE KRAKOW

A city where religion and culture have long had the upper hand over trade and commerce, Krakow is in many ways Poland's soul. Respect for the past keeps it anchored firmly in tradition, while its thousands of students keep it young.

At once both a centre of European Catholicism and Jewry, Krakow is nothing if not one giant contradiction. At its heart is the only medieval town centre of Poland's major cities to survive the horrors of the 20th century, yet Krakow is nevertheless a forward-thinking and outward-looking city. A Unesco World Heritage city, it records nearly 9 million visitors each year – and at times it can feel as if they're all clustered on Wawel Hill. However, in reality the city is large enough to contain locals and tourists alike, with plenty of green space affording relief, particularly in the height of summer.

With the recently improved transport connections, Krakow is as good a base as any to explore the rest of southern Poland, and a number of places are accessible on easy day trips: the mountain resort of Zakopane, the former Nazi concentration camp at Auschwitz, the Wieliczka Salt Mine and the Socialist-Realist 'new town' of Nowa Huta. Slightly further afield are no fewer than six national parks, the industrial city of Katowice and Krakow's former rival, Tarnów, which has its own charm.

FORMER CAPITAL OF POLAND

The name Krakow comes from Prince Krak, or Grakh, ruler of the Lechici, a Western Slavic people who inhabited the Lesser Poland (Małopolska) region towards the end of the 7th century, and who is credited in some quarters as founding the city. It is, however, generally believed Krakow was founded in about AD 950 by merchants using it as a staging post on the Amber Road from the Baltic to the Adriatic. Amber, most European of gemstones, remains a must-buy souvenir on any trip to the city, yet while the stone has been crucial to the city's development, it was the more prosaic commodity salt (mined at nearby Wieliczka since the early 11th century) that first made Krakow rich.

Royal approval arrived a century or so later, in 1038, when Wawel Hill and its cathedral became the official residence of Polish kings. Kazimierz the Restorer moved the capital here from Gniezno shortly after. It would remain the seat of power in Poland – and the region – until the 16th century, and though since then Warsaw

Icons for sale   *The wonderfully preserved Main Market Square*

has claimed political primacy, Krakow remains the cultural and religious heart of Poland.

CULTURAL, RELIGIOUS HUB

The country's oldest university is in Krakow – the Jagellonian University, founded in 1364. In 1533 the Dominicans staged Poland's first play here, and about two and a half centuries later the country's first permanent theatre, the Stary, was built. In the late 19th century the Stary, and Krakow, were major players in the development of the Młoda Polska (Young Poland) movement of artists, architects, poets and dramatists, whose adaption of Art Nouveau, or Secession, styles became synonymous with the city. More recently, Krakow was one of the European Capitals of Culture chosen for the 2000 millennium.

As the city from which Karol Wojtyła (born in 1920 in Wadowice, 40km/25 miles southwest of Krakow) became Pope John Paul II in 1978, Krakow has since become a centre of Roman Catholic pilgrimage as important – to many Poles at least – as the Vatican itself. To the many Jews who visit, Krakow is an important place of remembrance: the wartime ghetto the Nazis established was one of Europe's largest, though the horrors of life within its walls pale into insignificance when the nearby site of Auschwitz is visited.

GEOGRAPHY, CLIMATE AND PEOPLE

Krakow sits more than 200m (700ft) above sea level at the foot of the Carpathian Mountains, and the larger city is split in two by the Wisła (Vistula), though the areas that tourists visit are neatly encircled by the river. A city of extreme weather, Krakow can be covered in snow for two or three months of the year (December to February), yet in July and August temperatures often climb to over

The Secession

The Secession was an influential movement in art and architecture, which from the late 1890s until the early 1920s had a profound and lasting impact on all territories of the former Austro-Hungarian Empire. Regarded as the Viennese branch of the contemporaneous Parisian Art Nouveau movement, Secessionism represented a return to the notion of art for art's sake after the realism, linearity and functionalism of the neoclassical movement. Originating in Vienna in 1897, the Secession spread quickly to Budapest, Bratislava and to Krakow, where it manifested itself primarily in the decorative architecture of the old city centre, and in Kazimierz. The Young Poland movement, led by Stanisław Wyspiańksi (see page 71), was very much influenced by the Secession.

Cracovian elder

30°C (86°F). Dress and plan your activities accordingly, and note that downpours are a frequent menace, even on the warmest days.

Home to some 755,000 people, Krakow is Poland's second-largest city. Nowadays, almost all of its inhabitants are Poles. Until 1941 and the Holocaust, the Jews were a significant ethnic group, making up a quarter of the city's population. Though some of the hundreds of thousands of Jews who visit each year are now staying on, fewer than a thousand call the city permanent home.

A CITY OF MANY SIGHTS

For a city born of trade, it is only fitting that the centre of Krakow is the sublime Main Market Square (Rynek Główny). Its centrepiece, the Cloth Hall, is for many as much a symbol of Krakow and its past as Wawel Cathedral. For most, it is the first stop on explorations of the Old Town, a grid of fascinating narrow streets. On the edge of the Main Market Square is the 13th-century St Mary's (Kościół Mariacki), Krakow's main civic church and a high Gothic reminder of the city's past. The prominence given to a statue of national poet Adam Mickiewicz is a sign of Krakow's links with Polish literature.

The Planty
Uniquely among Europe's older quarters, a green belt, the Planty, surrounds the Old Town and provides both respite and definition. It was laid out at the beginning of the 19th century to replace the by then redundant city walls, Krakow having long since expanded in all directions. The park is itself surrounded by a ring of major boulevards, beyond which the more modern parts of the city have their own attractions, not least Secession-era architecture.

Beyond the Old Town
There is much more to Krakow than the Old Town. Towering above all is Wawel Hill, where you will find an imposing castle and cathedral, adorned with some of Europe's finest artworks since medieval times. At its base is the district of Okół, likely the site of the first Krakow settlement. For a different side to the city, visit the ancient Jewish quarter of Kazimierz, outside the city walls and with its own distinctive character. Now experiencing a renaissance, it is the city's liveliest district and a popular haunt of students and bohemians, who throng its many bars and cafés.

West of the Old Town is Piasek, where fine old apartment buildings surround quiet, hidden courtyards. Rich Cracovians made their homes in Nowy Swiat (New Town) in the 19th century when the Old Town became too crowded. Across the river is the Jewish ghetto Podgórze, made famous by the film *Schindler's List*.

Lajkonik parade in full swing

John Paul II moved to Krakow in 1938

ENTERTAINMENT CENTRAL

Enormously popular with young visitors, and home for much of the year to a large student population, Krakow over the past decade has become famous for its nightlife. Its clubs and bars buzz with activity from dusk to dawn most nights of the week, though Krakow does not lack other kinds of entertainment. Cabaret, theatre, opera and music venues are dotted throughout the city.

DON'T LEAVE KRAKOW WITHOUT...

Sipping coffee in Lenin's haunt. The quintessential Secession café in Main Market Square, Noworolski has played host to many revolutionaries over the years. In time off from planning his revolution, Lenin could be seen taking it easy here. See page 24.

Finding the Poles' soul at Wawel. Artist Stanisław Wyspiański said of Wawel Castle and Cathedral that 'the person who enters here becomes a part of Poland'. So get to the heart of things and revel in this opulent royal complex. See page 36.

Tracing the story of Schindler. Explore Podgórze, Krakow's Jewish ghetto for two years during World War II, and then tour the Oskar Schindler Factory as it unfolds its harrowing tale. Visit the poignant memorial in the district's Heroes of the Ghetto Square. See page 80.

Viewing a masterpiece by Leonardo da Vinci. Why grapple with the queues to glimpse the *Mona Lisa* in Paris or *The Last Supper* in Milan when you can see a classic Leonardo da Vinci portrait in Krakow? The stunning *Lady with an Ermine*, on temporary display at Wawel Castle, will once again be at the Czarto-ryski Museum in the Old Town in 2015. See page 34.

Stepping inside beautiful St Mary's. Krakow's most famous landmark, St Mary's Basilica in Main Market Square, has an interior to take your breath away. Don't miss the remarkable altarpiece. See page 29.

Reliving the Soviet past. Gain insight into Poland's Communist years with a visit to the suburb of Nowa Huta. Amid the monumental Socialist Realist architecture is a church built by locals to resemble Noah's Ark. See page 84.

Trying the national tipple. Think vodka and think Russia, but the Poles lay equal claim to the invention of the drink and have many different varieties to sample. The best selection can be found in the historic Jewish district of Kazimierz, home to a lively nightlife scene. See page 42.

Seeing the works of a young genius. Polymath Stanisław Wyspiański was at the heart of the Młoda Polska (Young Poland) art movement. You can check his brilliance with his stained-glass work at St Francis on route 6 and follow his style at a museum dedicated to his work. See pages 55 and 70.

The exquisite domes of Wawel Cathedral

Fairs and festivals

Throughout the year a flurry of colourful fairs are held on Krakow's streets, none more so than the blessing of palms on Palm Sunday. On Easter Monday, the Emmaus Fair in Zwiernyniec Park brings a colourful end to the Holy Week, while Corpus Christi is marked with a parade from Wawel to Main Market Square, and followed by the popular Lajkonik parade from Salwator the following Thursday. In December, stalls selling delicious local treats and gifts fill the Main Market Square. There are many other more modern festivals dedicated to all sorts of things, from sea shanties to soup, and even dachshunds.

Dining out

Krakow has a deserved reputation as a great place to eat out. While Polish cuisine itself is not generally regarded as being particularly sophisticated, Krakow has benefited from the influences of the Hapsburg Empire, with Viennese and Hungarian specialities finding their way onto the city's menus, frequently in the form of tasty local versions. Look out for game dishes such as *kaczka* (duck) and *dzik* (wild boar). Most waiting staff in Krakow speak fairly good English, and usually a smattering of German, too; many are students subsidising their studies. Menus can usually be found in English (of a sort), and staff never seem to mind helping out.

THE CITY'S FUTURE

Krakow is looking forward to the next decade with confidence, boosted by investment in the transport system. Due for completion in 2015, the airport is the subject of huge investment, enlarging to three times the size, with an additional terminal, Hilton hotel and new railway station. Roads, including the A4 motorway, as well as rail links will be improved to whisk visitors to the city. With its new capacity the airport will be well able to cope with the recent increase in tourist numbers and this has attracted budget airline Ryanair to set up base here and invest heavily in the project.

Plenty has been going on in central Krakow, too. The second stage of the 'New City' project is underway with major investment in hotels, office blocks and apartments. The city's main railway station, Krakow Główny, opened its new ticket hall and amenities in 2014, with further refurbishment to come. It has Poland's first underground railway interchange, with direct access to the redeveloped bus station. Further modernisation of tramlines has also been implemented. New buildings include the ICE Congress Centre and a new sports stadium east of the centre. Krakow's historic buildings are not being forgotten, with a major long-term programme of restoration in progress.

After making its mark as City of Literature in 2013, Krakow now has its sights on the 2022 Winter Olympics. A bid for

Oskar Schindler's former factory is now a modern museum

the games was made in late 2013 and a decision on who will host the games will be decided in Kuala Lumpur, Malaysia in July 2015.

TOP TIPS FOR VISITING KRAKOW

Stay in Kazimierz. The city's Jewish quarter is as lively during the evening – if not more so – as it is during the day. For the full Kazimierz experience, you can stay in one of the area's hotels; a few offer a full kosher package (see page 106).

Synagogue visits. As the last functioning synagogue in Kazimierz, Remuh is strict about men covering their heads and women their arms when visiting, as is the New Jewish Cemetery. While in Kazimierz's bohemian bars anything goes fashion-wise, it makes sense to dress appropriately for church and synagogue visiting.

Snack time. Look out for stalls selling street food including obwarzanki (pretzel-like bread rings flavoured with rock salt or poppy seeds) and świderki (literally 'little drills' – sweet, brioche-style bread fingers). Also popular are kiełbasa (rich sausages served with sweet mustard and a slice of bread) and zapiekanki (a kind of Polish pizza made of sliced baguette topped with cheese, mushrooms and ketchup).

Unlicensed cabs. Top-range hotels will often attract the attention of unlicensed cab drivers, so avoid rip-offs by making sure any taxi you use is clearly marked with its rates displayed on the window. Also be aware that some of the better-class hotels use their own official taxis, which will also often charge well above and beyond the going rate. Nasty surprises can be avoided by arranging a fee beforehand, or asking reception to call a reputable company.

What to wear. Krakow is a great city to explore on foot, so comfortable walking shoes are essential. Bring warm clothes if you're visiting in winter, as the weather can be very chilly, and remember to have something waterproof (or at least an umbrella) with you in spring or autumn, as showers are quite common.

Alfresco at a price. Note that many venues operate a dual pricing policy, with higher prices (or a simple surcharge) being applied to those sitting outside. Check before ordering.

Local guides. There are hundreds of local guides touting their trade, though not all are good. Recommended is Agnieszka Drzaszcz, tel: 060 021 24 98; www.krakowguide.pl. For good in-depth local knowledge try the Free Walking Tour; www.freewalkingtour.com.

Krakow Tourist Card. To save time and money pick up the two- (75zł) or three-day (95zł) Tourist Card, which entitles you to free travel on city buses and trams (day and night), and free entry in up to 30 Krakow museums. The card also offers discounts at selected restaurants and shops as well as excursions. It is available at all tourist information offices and online – for a full list of vendors and benefits visit www.krakowcard.com.

The Christmas Market in Main Market Square

FOOD AND DRINK

Polish food, based on simple ingredients and distinctive flavours, is both hearty and tasty. In Krakow, local specialities are complemented by a wide range of international restaurants serving fine cuisine.

You will not go hungry here. The city's range of good restaurants continues to expand, and, with a number of the better hotels hiring top chefs to oversee their kitchens, you can expect good quality, though often at a price. Many Old Town restaurants are expensive, though visitors on tighter budgets will always find *pierogi* – classic Polish dumplings – in plentiful supply. Krakow is synonymous with coffee culture, and there are small independent cafés and patisseries all over the city, with few examples of the global coffee chains ubiquitous elsewhere.

Menus are available in English and German in most Old Town restaurants, and in many more besides. Poles love to dine alfresco, and the city's restaurants and cafés have outside tables as soon as it is warm enough.

POLISH SPECIALITIES

Pork, potatoes and cabbage are the country's staples, and the national dish is *bigos*, a chunky stew of pork, other meats and sausages, cabbage, potatoes and onions, spiced with herbs and served with lashings of sour cream. Though it originates in eastern Poland, where winters are long, it is found everywhere. *Pierogi* are small, semicircular ravioli-like dumplings stuffed with meat, cheese or sometimes fruit. You can pick them up from any of the numerous inexpensive *pierogi* bars. Look out, too, for *barscz*, a delicious red beetroot soup flavoured with lemon and garlic and served hot or cold. Home-made chicken soup is another great Polish favourite.

Given that the forests and lakes to the south and east of Krakow are full of game, the local penchant for pheasant, duck (often roasted and served with apples), venison and boar is understandable. Autumn is the best time to try game dishes, which are served with rich

Pierogi, a Polish speciality   *Enjoying alfresco drinks*

sauces and vegetables. Polish sausages are excellent, with the heavily smoked *Gruba Krakowska* a local speciality.

Snacks and sweets

For snacks, look out for *precel* stalls selling hot and vaguely sweet pretzels (also known as *obwazanki*), usually topped with salt, or *zapiekanki*, a Polish version of pizza, with the topping piled on a halved baguette. Polish desserts, such as *kremówka*, cream cakes often covered in honey, are very sweet.

INTERNATIONAL CUISINE

Some of Poland's best restaurants are in Krakow, which has a range of cuisines to rival any city in Europe; from cutting-edge Modern European to Pacific Rim Fusion, new flavours are forever being created in the city's best kitchens. Catering for the large numbers of Jewish visitors, there is a good range of Jewish restaurants, centred on Kazimierz, although not all are strictly kosher. There are good Indian and Italian restaurants and some super German-owned beer halls selling sausages with lashings of sauerkraut. There is a better choice for vegetarians than in many other places in this part of Europe.

DRINKS

Vodka is the national spirit but beer is the more popular day-to-day drink, and it's both cheap and mostly good. Good popular local brews are Tyskie, Warka and Żywiec, and all have a crisp and refreshing taste. Imported beers, especially Heineken and Stella Artois, are now far more popular with trendy locals, however. Guinness is widely available, not just in the many Irish pubs, but is relatively expensive. Poland has a burgeoning wine industry, but most wines sold in restaurants and bars are imported. Poles love wine, however, so there is usually a good selection on offer. Coffee is preferred to tea, which is seen as a medicinal drink.

Café culture

In Krakow, coffee (and the café) is king – a legacy of the Hapsburg period. Locals will visit a café on their way to work, at lunchtime and on their way home. Yet café culture in Krakow is much more than drinking coffee: the city's cafés are debating chambers, reading rooms and places of inspiration.

Vodka

Poles boast that they invented vodka, in the 14th century, though the other countries of the grain-growing region of eastern Poland, southern Lithuania, Belarus and Russia have equal claims. Made from water and either grain, molasses, potatoes or sugar beet, vodka was first used as a medicine, becoming a recreational drink in the 16th century. The best-known brand is *Wyborowa*, while flavoured blends include *Goldwasser*, *Starka* and *Żubrówka* (Bison Grass Vodka).

Setting the mood

ENTERTAINMENT

Krakow is Poland's cultural capital and home to its liveliest nightlife. From the theatre of the Old Town to Kazimierz's trendy bars – many of which stay open 'until the last guest leaves' – there is something for everyone.

When it comes to things to do when the sun goes down in Krakow, most people find themselves spoilt for choice. From young clubbers, who can dance until dawn in one of the city's many nightspots that cater to fans of every music genre – to sophisticated city breakers forced to choose between the philharmonic and the opera, there is plenty of everything for everyone. Cinephiles and sports fans have lots of options, too. This section gives an overview of the entertainment options on offer; for more detailed listings, see page 122.

THEATRE AND CABARET

The Narodowy Stary Teatr (see page 122) is the oldest theatre in Poland and here you can see the country's best stage actors. Even if you are not attending a play, both the Stary and the Juliusz Słowacki Theatre (see page 122) are worth visiting to admire their sumptuous interiors.

There is also a century-long history of cabaret in Krakow that continues today. The best (and most regular) are those at the Piwnica pod Baranami (see page 122) basement club.

MUSIC AND OPERA

The city's Szymanowski Philharmonic Orchestra (named after the celebrated late 19th-century/early 20th-century Polish composer and pianist) performs at the grand concert hall of the same name (see page 122), a cavernous venue that welcomes international musicians and has an often adventurous artistic policy. Krakow's opera (Opera Krakowska, see page 122) for years suffered from a lack of a permanent home, but in 2008 took possession of its own new premises.

Jazz

Jazz fans are in for a treat in Krakow; the Jazz Club u Muniaka (see page 122) is one of the best in Europe. Celebrated Polish and international jazzmen play every Friday and Saturday night. Look out, too, for Harris Piano Jazz Bar (see page 122), a jazz and blues club whose cellar always seems full.

NIGHTLIFE

It is claimed that Krakow's Old Town has more pubs per square mile than

Krakow brims with jazz clubs   *Cocktail time*

any other city in Europe, so make sure you seek out only the very best on offer. Krakow's endless charm lies in exploring its bountiful bar scene. The line between bars and cafés remains blurred, and nowhere is this truer than in the Kazimierz district, where shadowy locales, buried in nostalgia and candlelight, transform into havens of hedonism as evening progresses. Tested favourites are: the C.K. Browar beer hall (see page 123) for a raucous pint with locals and visitors; and trendy Movida (see page 123) for a more sophisticated evening sipping cocktails.

You should also head to Kazimierz for at least a couple of drinks, and try out one or two of the bars around Plac Nowy. Le Scandale (pl. Nowy 9; www.lescandale.pl) serves great cocktails, while candle-lit Alchemia (see page 122), with a separate space for live music, is a Kazimierz institution.

Clubbing

Clubbing in Krakow once meant squelching across floors while the foundations shook to unimaginative chart noise. The city has grown up, however, and while the lion's share of clubs can still be found in the vaulted catacombs of Krakow's cellars, adding some disco lights and a bedroom DJ is no longer enough. Divey, lager-in-a-plastic-glass student clubs are still in abundance, but so too are cutting-edge dance floors employing dress-to-impress gate policies.

Make your first stop Cień (see page 123), as everybody else does. A little more select are Baccarat (see page 123), a place the city's beautiful set has made its own, and Fusion Club (ul. Floriańska 15; www.clubfusion.ivn.pl), where only the best-dressed and trendiest are selected for entry.

CINEMA

In the centre of Krakow the fine old Sztuka movie hall on ul. św Jana 6 dates from 1916 and now shows Hollywoood blockbusters under the ARS banner (see page 123). Multi-screen cinemas include the enormous Cinema City (see page 123) at the Krakow Plaza shopping centre east of the city. Films are usually shown in their original language with Polish subtitles.

Football

Krakow, like most of Poland, is football crazy, with the local teams Wisła Krakow and Cracovia having competed with the best in the Polish league. The two home teams, which occupy impressive new stadia facing each other across the Błonie, enjoy long-standing rivalry, dubbed the 'Holy War'. Though games are well attended they are not usually sell-outs, so getting a ticket should be easy. The season runs from July to May, with a break in December and January.

Ul. Grodzka is a good place to head for boutiques

SHOPPING

While never hoping to rival London, Paris, or even Warsaw, as a shopping destination, Krakow offers plenty to spend your money on, with its modern shopping centres, small boutiques and specialist stores.

Nobody comes to Krakow to shop, but treasures can be found in the city. Beyond Hapsburg antiques and the ubiquitous amber, you should look out for leather goods and accessories, tableware, glassware and lace.

CLOTH HALL AND THE MARKETS

The first stop for many visitors – shopping or not – the Cloth Hall offers a wide selection of the kind of souvenirs you will find throughout the city and prices are much the same as elsewhere. Look out for good-quality folk art, carved wooden sculptures and toys and tasteful religious art, as well as modern jewellery and amber, which has been traded here since the city began. Krakow's other markets tend to sell produce only, but are great if you want to see people going about their daily business. The largest, Hala Targowa, with a flea market on Sunday mornings, is that on ul. Grzegórzecka, a short walk east of the city centre. There's a small weekend flea market in Kazimierz in Plac Nowy, while Rynek Kleparski, just north of the Old Town, is a handy market for buying cheese, sausage, bread and other picnic supplies. In December, the Christmas Market in Rynek Główny (Main Market Square) fills the square with stalls selling hand-made goods and delicious hot local snacks.

SHOPPING STREETS

The main shopping thoroughfares in the centre are ul. Floriańska, the Main Market Square and ul. Grodzka, which link up to form a 'shopping triangle'. It can be difficult to recommend specific outlets: it's not uncommon for shops to have no street number and some stores, in keeping with the Communist legacy, display only generic titles such as 'Jeweller', with no clear name.

Two big, modern shopping centres are within easy reach of the Old Town: Galeria Krakowska (www.galeriakrakowska.pl), opposite the main railway station, and Galeria Kazimierz (www.galeriakazimierz.pl), on the outskirts of Kazimierz and well served by buses and trams to Rondo Grzegórzeckie.

Opening hours

Typical hours are Mon–Fri 9/10am–7pm, Sat 9/10am–6pm (although some

Amber is plentiful

close at 1pm). Small shops are closed on Sunday, but big shopping centres open late. Most accept credit cards.

WHAT TO BUY

Clothes and jewellery

Leather goods including handbags, gloves, coats and luggage are all worth taking a look at. Fur hats, sheepskin coats, jackets and accessories are widely available, which may shock visitors from countries where wearing fur is a definite no-no. In Poland wearing fur coats and hats is very standard during the snowy winters.

Items made from amber often represent exceptionally good value, whether in the form of rings, earrings, necklaces, bracelets, cuff-links, or even bowls and jewellery boxes. You will have no trouble finding amber in Krakow: the best is in the small shops of the Old Town, such as Boruni, in the Cloth Hall and ul. Grodzka 60.

Antiques

An array of small shops sell all sorts of wonderful knick-knacks, from Soviet- and Nazi-era memorabilia to antique watches and clocks. While, technically, you cannot export items produced before 1945 – unless you gain prior written permission from the appropriate government department – small personal items such as medals, badges, watches and pens are usually exempt. Reputable antique shops can arrange authorisation and onward

shipping, but often at a cost. If you don't know where to begin, look in Galeria Osobliwości Este, a cabinet of curiosities at ul. Sławskowska 16, marked by a rhino skull hanging in the street, or browse in one of the most established shops in the Old Town, the upscale Salon Antyków at ul. Jagiellońska 9.

Sweets and vodka

Confectionery made at the famous Krakow Wawel sweet factory is a good buy, as is the generally excellent Polish vodka. Note that with vodka, price is directly related to quality.

Baltic gold

Amber, Poland's national gem stone, is fossilised tree resin that once seeped from deciduous and coniferous trees, solidified and, over the course of thousands of years, matured into the form we are familiar with today. This resin sometimes traps insects and flora, and amber that contains identifiable specimens of prehistoric life is considered a special rarity, and priced accordingly. The Baltic Sea washes up amber from beneath the surface of the sand, depositing it conveniently on beaches to be collected. The colour of the translucent stone ranges across a surprising spectrum, from the more common yellow and white to stones with red and green streaks and tinges. These tints aren't flaws; they add character to the stone.

Mythical dragon of Wawel Hill

HISTORY: KEY DATES

With a rich but much troubled history, Krakow still bears some of the scars from battles fought over its cultural and religious landmarks. Most have fortunately, miraculously even, survived.

EARLY TO MEDIEVAL KRAKOW

50,000 BC	First known settlement on Wawel Hill, Palaeolithic era.
9th cent. AD	Wawel Hill becomes a fortified village and the seat of the Wiślan (Vistulan) Dukes.
965	The earliest written reference to Krakow, by a Spanish merchant, describes 'a major town known throughout Europe'.
1000	The bishopric of Krakow is founded following Poland's conversion to Christianity in 966.
1038	King Kazimierz Odnowiciel (Casimir the Restorer) moves the capital of Poland from Gniezno to Krakow and builds a royal residence on Wawel Hill.
1079	St Andrew's, one of Poland's earliest Romanesque churches, founded.
12th cent.	Wieliczka salt mine is established outside Krakow.
1241	Tartars destroy the town.
1257	Krakow gains municipal rights.
1290	Construction of St Mary's Basilica begins.
1335	Kazimierz is established as a separate town outside Krakow.
1364	Krakow hosts an international meeting of monarchs.
1386	The Grand Duke of Lithuania marries Queen Jadwiga of Poland, becoming King Władysław II Jagiello and joining the two countries with Krakow as the capital.
1400	Collegium Maius is established as the second university college in Central and Eastern Europe.

RENAISSANCE TO THE HAPSBURGS

1499	The Barbican is completed.
1556–60	The Cloth Hall is built in Renaissance style.

Karol Wojtyła's 1978 election as pope

1596	King Zygmunt III Waza transfers the royal residence to Warsaw, which he declares the capital of Poland.
1665–7	Swedish invaders ravage and loot the town.
1734	King Augustus III becomes the last Polish monarch to be crowned in Wawel Cathedral.
1783	Krakow's Botanical Gardens are established.
1791	Kazimierz becomes part of Krakow.
1796	After three successive partitions of Poland, Krakow becomes part of the Austro-Hungarian Empire.
1799	Poland's longest-serving theatre, Stary Teatr, is established.
1820s	The Planty gardens are laid out.
1846	Krakow leads an uprising against the Austro-Hungarian Empire.
1850	The Great Fire devastates the town's historic centre.
1879	Poland's first national museum is established in the Cloth Hall.

20TH CENTURY TO THE PRESENT

1918	Krakow becomes part of a newly independent Poland.
1939	Nazis establish administrative headquarters in the city.
1945	Red Army takes over Krakow leading to Communist, Soviet-satellite government of Poland.
1947–9	The Lenin Steelworks are built in the new suburb of Nowa Huta.
1978	Krakow's historic centre gains Unesco World Heritage Status; Cardinal Karol Wojtyła, Bishop of Krakow, is elected pope.
1981–3	Martial law declared in Poland.
1989	Democratic elections see free trade union Solidarity win.
2000	Krakow is declared a European City of Culture.
2004	Poland joins the European Union.
2007	The 750th anniversary of Krakow as a city.
2010	The body of Polish President Lech Kaczynski is interred at Wawel, after his death in the Smolensk plane crash.
2011	Pope John Paul II beatified; Poland takes over presidency of the EU for the first time.
2013	Krakow is officially designated Unesco's City of Literature. The city bids for the 2022 Winter Olympics.
2014	Poland commemorates the 70th anniversary of the Warsaw Uprising.
2015	The 70th anniversary of the liberation of Auschwitz.

A TA RĘKA WYR
— **KAROLA**

przy ulicy św. Gertrud

poleca Atramenta w 17 gatunkach do

c (czernidło) Indigowo - oliwny i

(lakiery) w trzech j

a obuwie damskie i dziecięce, c

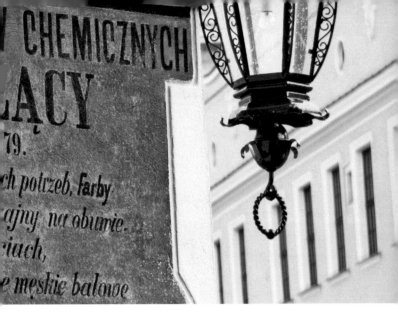

BEST ROUTES

Alfresco cafés line the Main Market Square

MAIN MARKET SQUARE

Playing heart to Wawel's soul, the Main Market Square has been Krakow's commercial and social centre for centuries. Every building has a story and in many cases great historical importance; all visits to Krakow should start here.

DISTANCE: 1km (0.6 mile)

TIME: A half day

START: In front of St Mary's

END: St Barbara's Church

POINTS TO NOTE: The houses in Main Market Square are numbered clockwise from St Mary's (no. 4; Cloth Hall is 1–3). Try to begin this route as early in the day as possible, but note that during summer months even a 7am start will not spare you the crowds. After completing this walk at St Mary's you can extend it by following route 2. To get an idea of the city's layout and for great panoramic views, climb to the top of the Town Hall Tower or St Mary's Watchtower.

Laid out in 1257 and measuring nearly 40,000sq m (10 acres), Krakow's **Main Market Square** (Rynek Główny) is one of Europe's largest medieval squares. It was once the scene of majestic royal parades, and official guests are still ceremoniously greeted here. On a more everyday level, the square has long been a thriving centre of commercial activity, and continues to bustle with locals and tourists. It is from here you can take horse-drawn carriage rides of the city.

In summer the buzz goes on late into the night. An abundance of cafés, restaurants, shops, flower stalls and street performers form a colourful, engaging atmosphere.

BURGHERS' HOUSES AND PALACES

The imposing burghers' houses and the grand palaces surrounding the Main Market Square were once owned by the city's wealthiest merchants and aristocratic families, and a variety of facades reflect diverse architectural genres.

Begin your walk at no. 4 (the first house on the square to the left of St Mary's). The house's upper levels are in Secessionist style, redesigned at the start of the 20th century, though the house is much older.

Cross ul. Sienna: to the left at no. 7 is the **Montelupi** or **Italian House** (Kami-

House under the Painting

enica Montelupich), the site of Poland's first post office, which operated from here in the 16th and 17th centuries. Mail coaches would enter the rear courtyard through the narrow arch. At no. 9, **Boner House** (Kamienica Bonerowska) has retained the original ornamental attic built in the 1560s, when the house belonged to the king's private banker, Jan Boner. **Bar 13** (see page 113), on the corner of the square, is a great coffee and cake location for a little early-morning pick me up before moving on.

ST ADALBERT'S

In the far southeastern corner of the square, and set slightly below current ground level, little **St Adalbert's Church** ❶ (Kościół św Wojciecha; Mon–Sat 9am–5pm and till 6pm in summer, Sun 1.30–6pm) dates back to the early 12th century. This tiny Romanesque church, resembling an elegant white cube with a Gothic cupola, has room for only a few pews. Nevertheless, its impressive interior features frescoes combining restraint and detailed ornamentation, including one of St Adalbert being killed by the Prussians after trying to convert them in AD 997.

The vaults

The vaults of St Adalbert's house a small exhibition on the history of the square (www.ma.krakow.pl; June-Oct, Mon–Sat 10am–4pm, closed Sun and win-

ter months; charge, free Mon). Here, visitors can see Romanesque and pre-Romanesque fragments of an even larger stone church, the remnants of a wooden church believed to be the first in Krakow, and the wooden remains of an even earlier pagan temple on display.

THE SOUTHERN FACADE

The city's most historic restaurant, **Wierzynek**, behind St Adalbert's and to the right at no. 15, comprises two Renaissance houses. One of the dining rooms features original 14th-century Gothic arches, and the wine bar and grill is situated in a 14th-century cellar (see page 118). The 17th-century **House Under the Painting** (Dom Pod Obrazem) at no. 19 features a beautiful fresco of the Blessed Virgin Mary ascending into heaven, completed in 1718. On the ground floor, **Słodki Wentzl** (see page 118) sells Krakow's best ice cream. The **Zbaraski Palace** at no. 20, which houses the Goethe Institute, was built in the 14th century, though its neoclassical facade dates from the 18th century, when the arcaded courtyard was added.

Following the square around to the western facade, the 14th century **Pałac Pod Baranami** (Palace Under the Rams) at no. 27 was refashioned in the mid-19th century. The courtyard garden is now a café, see ❶, and the Cellar Under the Rams (Piwnica Pod Baranami), a cabaret and music venue.

The cupola of St Adalbert's

Its founder Piotr Skryznecki is honoured with a statue in front of the **Vis-à-Vis** bar next door, see .

TOWN HALL TOWER

Opposite Vis-à-Vis is all that remains of the magnificent **Town Hall** ❷ (Ratusz): the **Town Hall Tower** (Wieża Ratuszowa; tel: 012 619 23 18; Apr–Oct daily 10.30am–5pm; charge). This handsome 70m- (230ft) high red-brick tower is inlaid with decorative stone and is principally 14th-century Gothic, with 16th-century Renaissance additions. The main town hall was demolished in 1820, at the same time as much of the city's defensive walls and towers, and it was only due to sustained protests by prominent locals that the tower was saved. It doesn't take long to view the tower (and much of that time is spent negotiating steep, narrow stairs). Beside the Town Hall Tower is a large modern sculpture of a head on its side that children like to climb; this is Eros Bendato by Igor Mitoraj (1944–), who studied at Krakow's Academy of Art.

Exhibitions

The first floor of the tower, originally a chapel, houses a collection of architectural fragments, though it is now mainly used for exhibitions. The third floor's photographic exhibition shows how the tower looked during the 19th century, and the top floor offers excellent views of Krakow. Visitors can also admire the old clock mechanism, which is now synchronised with the atomic clock.

MUSEUM OF THE CITY OF KRAKOW

Towards the northern side of the square on leaving the tower, the last building on the left is the **Krzysztofory Palace** ❸ (Pałac Krzysztofory; Rynek Główny 35; www.mhk.pl; Wed–Sat 10am–5.30pm; charge), which dates from the 17th century and houses the main offices of the of the of the MHK (Muzeum Historyczne Miasta Krakowa), which oversees many of the museums in the city. It also hosts temporary exhibitions. The opulent Fontana Room, still open to the public for concerts and other special occasions, has fine plasterwork by Baldassere Fontana from the end of the 17th century, which is worth seeing.

Next door at no. 34 is **Hawełka**, one of the city's most enduring restaurants, great for lunch or dinner (see page 115).

THE NORTHERN FACADE

Though the northern facade is less impressive than the square's other facades, the Baroque **Deer House** at no. 36, once an inn, and the classic town houses at nos 38 and 39 are worthy of inspection. The **Phoenix House** at no. 41 is home to the excellent **Loża Klub Aktora** café, see .

The Town Hall, Cloth Hall and St Adalbert's at dusk

The Bonerowski Palace Hotel, (see page 103), on the corner of ul. św Jana, was once another possession of the wealthy Boner family. Later it became the home and gallery of Feliks Jasieński (1861–1929), an influential 19th-century art collector.

At no. 47 is **Rynek Główny**, which sports a wonderful, oversized entrance and was once a mint. Today, fittingly, it is a bank,

CLOTH HALL

At the centre of Main Market Square is the magnificent **Cloth Hall ❹** (Sukiennice; Mon–Sat 10am–8pm, Sun 10am–6pm). Originally a covered market with stalls, shops and warehouses selling cloth and textiles, a building was first erected here in the mid-13th century. After the hall was almost destroyed by fire, Giovanni Maria of Padua (known as Padovano) designed the current Renaissance facade, including the loggias at either end, in 1556–60. The ornamental attic, decorated with mascarons for which Krakow's most distinguished burghers apparently posed, was the work of Santi Gucci of Florence. The roof also features copper globes surmounting small spires. During recent renovations it was discovered that these globes contained historical documents from the late 18th to the mid-19th century – there is a long tradition of builders secreting items for posterity in such 'time capsules'.

In the period immediately after World War II, plans were drawn up by Poland's newly installed Communist authorities to give the square a more proletarian look by ripping down Cloth Hall and replacing it with a Modernist Town Hall. Fortunately, good sense prevailed and the Cloth Hall survived.

Ground floor

The ground floor of the Sukiennice retains its commercial role. Stalls here sell folk arts and crafts, amber and silver jewellery, leather goods and good-quality souvenirs. The arcades added in 1875–9 on either side of the building now house attractive cafés. A delightful example, at no. 1, is the Secessionist-style **Kawiarnia Noworolski**, see ❶.

First-floor gallery

On the first floor of the Sukiennice, the **Gallery of 19th-Century Polish Painting and Sculpture** (Galeria Sztuki Polskiej XIX Wieku; www.muzeum.krakow.pl; Tue–Thu, Sun 10am–6pm, Fri–Sat 10am–8pm; charge) was Poland's first national museum. When it opened in 1879, Jan Matejko, the finest painter in the country's history, was among the artists who donated their own work. In addition to the works of Polish artists such as Matejko, Adam Chmielowski, J. Tatarkiewicz and P. Weloński, the collection features foreign artists in Poland, including the Italian Marcello Bacciarelli. You will also find the Tourist Information Centre on this floor.

Cloth Hall sculpture

RYNEK UNDERGROUND

The Krakow we see above ground looks old enough, but this exhibition (Podziemia Rynku; www.podziemiarynku.com; Mon 10am–8pm, Tue 10am–4pm, Wed–Sun 10am–10pm but till 8pm only Nov–Mar, closed first Tue in the month; charge, free Mon), which opened in 2010, traces its history back to the Celts and beyond. From the entrance on St Mary's side of the Cloth Hall, descend 4m (13ft) under the square to see artefacts excavated during the renovation of the Main Market Square, which provided evidence of 800 years of uninterrupted trade on this site. Both adults and children can enjoy interactive multimedia displays (visitors can select their language of choice) showing Krakow's place at the heart of European life from the 10th to the 14th centuries.

ADAM MICKIEWICZ MONUMENT

Directly outside the Sukiennice in the Main Market Square is the **Adam Mickiewicz Monument** ❺ (Pomnik Adama Mickiewicza), a popular meeting point for locals. It honours Poland's greatest romantic poet, Adam Mickiewicz (see box). Designed by Teodor Rygier, it was unveiled in 1898 on the centenary of the poet's birth. Mickiewicz never actually visited Krakow, at least not during his lifetime. On the 35th anniversary of his death his body was brought here and placed in Wawel Cathedral crypt. The monument is the venue for Krakow's popular pre-Christmas crib *(szopki)* competition. On the first Thursday of December exquisitely decorated *szopki* are brought to the square by amateur craftsmen from all over Lesser Poland. The winning cribs are displayed in the Museum of the City of Krakow.

Other traditional events held in Main Market Square include the colourful

Adam Mickiewicz

Few poets have the honour of being declared a nation's eternal poet; Adam Mickiewicz (1798–1855) is probably unique in having had the honour bestowed on him in two countries. For just as Mickiewicz is adored in his adopted Poland, so he is revered in Lithuania, the country of his birth, and where he is known as Adomas Mickevičius. His nationality is therefore a moot point, and in these parts a touchy subject. While he is undisputedly a Polish poet (he wrote exclusively in Polish), his ethnicity is in fact unknown, and both Poles and Lithuanians claim him as their own. In fact, evidence suggests that he might well have been of either Belarussian or even Tartar stock. The fact that his most famous poem – Pan Tadeusz, written of course in Polish – begins with the line 'O Lithuania, My Fatherland…' only confuses things further.

City museum exhibits   *Veit Stoss's triptych, St Mary's*

Lajkonik pageant shortly after Corpus Christi. This sees a procession of people dressed as Tartars marching through the streets led by the *Lajkonik* – according to legend, one of the Vistula River rafters disguised as a Tartar riding a hobby-horse that dances to the beat of accompanying drums. It's considered good luck to be touched by the *Lajkonik*'s wooden mace.

ST MARY'S

The most important building in the Main Market Square is the imposing, twin-towered **St Mary's Basilica** ❻ (Kościół Mariacki; Mon–Sat 11.30am–6pm, Sun 2–6pm; ceremonial opening of the high altar, daily except Sun 11.50am). This church has two entrances, one for tourists at the rear (charge), the other (the main entrance) for regular worshippers or for those (excluding tourists) attending Mass. Construction of this triple-naved Gothic basilica began in 1288, incorporating some fragments of an earlier Romanesque church that was burnt during the Tartar invasion of 1221.

St Mary's was privately funded and, according to the medieval Polish chronicler Jan Długosz, it immedi-

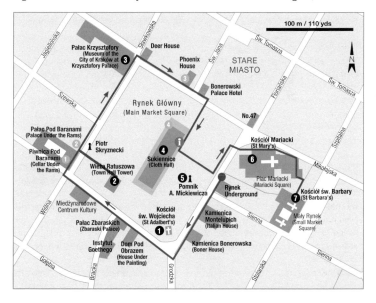

Adam Mickiewicz statue

ately became the city's principal parish church. The side chapels and towers were only completed in the early 14th century. The shorter of the two is the bell tower; the other, more ornamental tower bears a late-Baroque 'crown' on the spire dedicated to the Virgin Mary, and served as a city watchtower.

The beautiful, intricate interiors, dating variously from the Gothic, Renaissance and Baroque eras, repay a leisurely visit. The late 19th-century polychromy was designed by leading Polish artists, including Jan Matejko and Stanisław Wyspiański, with the stained-glass windows also designed by Wyspiański and Józef Mehoffer.

Veit Stoss's masterpiece

The church's most extraordinary work of art is the late Gothic triptych altarpiece entitled *The Lives of Our Lady and Her Son Jesus Christ*. This was completed between 1477 and 1489 by the Nuremberg master carver Veit Stoss (known in Poland as Wit Stwosz), who was considered the finest craftsman of his age.

The altarpiece incorporates over 200 carved figures (many of them based on contemporary Cracovians) and decorative elements made from linden wood. The central panel, 13m (42ft) high and 11m (36ft) wide, and opened every day at 11.50am, depicts the Virgin Mary falling into an eternal sleep, surrounded by the Apostles. It is considered perhaps the finest piece of Polish sculpture ever executed. Side panels depict scenes from the life of the Virgin Mary and Jesus.

Incredibly, a shift in artistic trends during the 17th century saw an attempt to replace the masterpiece with a plasterwork sculpture: only the Swedish invasion of 1655 prevented its total destruction, though part – it was originally much larger – was lost for ever.

Another Stoss masterpiece, a stone cross known as the *Slacker Crucifix* and depicting Christ in some discomfort on the cross, can be seen in the south aisle. After completing the cross and altarpiece, Stoss remained in Krakow, where he worked for the king as well as a number of aristocrats for a further 20 years.

The trumpeter

Every hour, on the hour, day and night, a trumpeter from the local fire brigade plays the *hejnał*, a short tune, from the taller **tower**. This tradition originates from the time a watchman, seeing the Tartars prepare to scale the city walls at dawn, blew his trumpet to raise the alarm. The Tartars fired a salvo of arrows at the watchman and after a few notes he was hit in the throat. Although the tune was cut off in mid-melody, the town was roused from sleep and defended itself.

In memory of this event, the *hejnał* is played four times on every hour (to the four sides of the world) and every time it is stopped abruptly.

Stained glass in St Mary's

St Barbara's ceiling

ST BARBARA'S

Behind St Mary's Basilica on **Mariacki Square** (Plac Mariacki), laid out at the beginning of the 18th century on the site of the former parish cemetery, is **St Barbara's Church ❼** (Kościół św Barbary). Apparently the church was constructed with the materials left from the construction of St Mary's, and by the same craftsmen. It originated in 1338 as the cemetery chapel. The small façade features a Renaissance portal as well as 15th-century late Gothic sculptures depicting Christ in the Garden of Gethsemane.

Sacral art

The Baroque interiors, effectively painted in two shades of blue, also include three Gothic works of sacral art – the *pietà* sculpture, a crucifix, and polychromy depicting the Apprehending of Christ. Additional polychromy on the vaulted ceiling was completed by Piotr Franciszek Molitor in 1765. The 17th-century main altar has paintings of the Virgin Mary and St Barbara (who died in 1621 and is buried in the crypt), plus a finely carved altar rail.

Chapel

The 17th-century Chapel of the Blessed Virgin Mary features the miraculous icon of Matka Boska Jurowicka (the Madonna of Jurowice), brought to Krakow in 1885 from the town of Jurowice, where the cult of the Blessed Virgin Mary developed.

Food and Drink

❶ PAŁAC POD BARANAMI

Rynek Główny 27 (Courtyard); tel: 012 422 01 77; Sun–Thu 5pm–2am, Fri–Sat 5pm–4am; €€

This is an Old Town legend of a café, bar and club. It is one of the few places in the Old Town just as popular with locals as visitors, and has a grit and authenticity that trendier newcomers lack.

❷ VIS-À-VIS

Rynek Główny 29; tel: 012 422 69 61; daily 8am–11pm; €€

Another Main Market Square café that is just as popular with locals as visitors, and as such is a great place to people-spot.

❸ LOZA KLUB AKTORA

Rynek Główny 41; tel: 012 429 29 62; www.loza.pl; daily 9am–2am; €€€

One of the newer breed of multi-purpose Krakow cafés, this place does a good range of sandwiches and cakes in the day, while later on it becomes a trendy drinking venue.

❹ KAWIARNIA NOWOROLSKI

Rynek Główny 1/3; tel: 012 422 47 71; daily 7am–midnight; €€€

Lenin allegedly drank coffee here, as did untold other revolutionaries and literary types who have so often made Krakow their home. The quintessential Krakow café.

Small Market Square

SKIRTING THE ROYAL ROUTE

When kingly processions would close the Royal Route, Cracovians would be forced to make lengthy detours. Starting at Small Market Square this route, packed with little gems and some of the best art and architecture in the city, follows one such detour back to Main Market Square.

DISTANCE: 1km (0.6 mile)
TIME: A half day
START: Small Market Square
END: Main Market Square
POINTS TO NOTE: Small Market Square is directly behind St Barbara's Church, which can be seen from Main Market Square. The main building of Czartoryski Museum is closed for renovation until 2015.

SMALL MARKET SQUARE

The start of our walk, the **Small Market Square ❶** (Mały Rynek), served as the city's meat market until the 19th century. Today it hosts some good cafés for a pre-walk primer, including **Albo Tak Café** at no. 4, see ❶.

Turn left at the square's northern end, on to Mikołajska, and you will see the **Kamienica Hipolitów** (Plac Mariacki 3; Apr–Oct Wed 10am–5pm, Thu–Sun until 5.30pm, Nov–Mar Wed, Fri–Sun 9am–4pm, Thu noon–7pm; charge, free Wed), a 17th-century building containing re-creations of interiors of burghers' houses from the 16th to the 20th centuries. Much of the fine furniture on display is original.

ST THOMAS THE APOSTLE AND THE HOLY CROSS

Exiting the Kamienica Hipolitów and taking a left, head 100 metres/yds north along ul. Szpitalna, where you'll come across the **Church of St Thomas the Apostle ❷** (Kościół św Tomasza Apostoła) at no. 12. This is a prime example of 17th-century Baroque architecture.

Continuing along ul. Szpitalna, you'll reach Plac św Ducha (Square of the Holy Spirit). On the right-hand corner of the square is the Dom Pod Krzyżem, a museum of Cracovian theatre (closed until 2016), but the square's real masterpiece is the Gothic **Holy Cross Church ❸** (Kościół św Kryża; ul. św Kryża 23) at the rear. The church's inner portal, the chapel of St Mary Magdalene and the baptismal font are fine examples of Gothic design. A chapel dedicated to the founder of the church, St Dominic, is one of the best

Florian's Gate　　　　　　　　*Inside the Kamienica Hipolitów*

examples of Polish Renaissance art. The impressive vaulted ceiling, supported by a single pillar, includes 16th-century polychromy with 19th-century additions by Stanisław Wyspiański. The Holy Cross Church is also known as the Actors' Church, and you can see an epitaph to the 19th-century Polish actress Helena Modrzejewska at the entrance.

JULIUSZ SŁOWACKI THEATRE

Opposite is the **Juliusz Słowacki Theatre ❹** (Teatr im J. Słowackiego; Plac św Ducha 1; www.slowacki.krakow.pl). One of the city's leading theatrical venues, this fabulously eclectic, neo-Renaissance gem was designed by Jan Zawiejski, who modelled it on the Paris Opéra. Built in 1893 on the site of a hospital, it features ornate interiors, including impressive stage curtains painted with allegories of comedy and tragedy.

FLORIAN'S GATE

Leave the square and continue north along ul. Szpitalna. Turn left into ul. Pijarska towards **Florian's Gate ❺** (Brama Floriańska). Once the main route to the north of the city, this is the only remaining gateway in the walls of the town's defences, which once included eight gates and almost 40 bastions.

The passageway within the gate features a small, mid-19th century altar with a Gothic painting of Our Lady Mary of Piaski. Part of the old city wall, together with four 14th-century bastions, extends on either side of Florian's Gate. This wall now serves as open-air exhibition space for local painters.

PIARISTS' CHURCH

Continue along ul. Pijarska. At the junction with ul. św Jana is the **Piarists' Church ❻** (Kościół Pijarów), one of the city's smallest and most fascinating churches. The Piarist Order first built a chapel and adjoining residence in Krakow in 1682, after the brothers had been asked to teach students of theology at the Jagiellonian University. The congregation grew to the extent that the chapel soon became too small, so Duke Hieronim Lubomirski acquired a neighbouring disused brewery for the Piarists. Wealthy Cracovians contributed to the building costs, and the new church was consecrated in 1728.

The interiors feature Eckstein and Hoffman's illusionist murals, modelled on those of St Ignatius' Church in Rome, while the vaulted ceiling and a depiction of Christ Ascending into Heaven (copied from Raphael) by the altar are particularly impressive. Every year during Holy Week a reproduction of Christ's Tomb is set up in the crypt of the Piarists' Church. The crypt is also sometimes a venue for exhibitions and theatre performances.

Should you wish to eat before heading any further, try the **Chłopskie Jadło** (see page 113), two minutes south along ul. św Jana on the corner of ul. św Marka.

The passageway within Florian's Gate

CZARTORYSKI MUSEUM

Opposite the Piarists' Church is one of the city's most important museums, **Czartoryski Museum** ❼ (Muzeum Czartoryskich; ul. św Jana 19; www.muzeum-czartoryskich.krakow.pl). Both this historic palace and the neighbouring monastery were acquired by the Czartoryski family in 1876 to display their magnificent art collection. The municipality donated the adjoining Renaissance Arsenal to provide further galleries. Together these buildings offer a period setting for a fine collection that includes 13th- to 16th-century Polish, German, Italian, Spanish, Flemish and Dutch masters, sculpture, sacral art and objets d'art, as well as ancient Roman, Greek and Egyptian art. An unusual feature is the collection of Turkish tents, suits of armour and other military effects acquired at the Battle of Vienna in 1683, when King Jan III Sobieski led the victorious charge against the Ottoman aggressors. The Polish haul included Turkish coffee cups – the first coffee drunk in Poland was taken from the Turkish pavilions.

The main building of the museum, the Gallery of European Painting, is closed for restoration until 2015. During this time one of the outstanding masterpieces of the collection, Leonardo da Vinci's *Lady with an Ermine*, (c.1480–90), bought by the Czartoryski family in 1800, has been loaned out to galleries in other countries and is now exhibited at the Wawel Royal Castle (see page 36). This prize exhibit was hidden from the Nazis at the outbreak of World War II, only to be found and made part of Hitler's personal art collection. It was returned to Krakow in 1946.

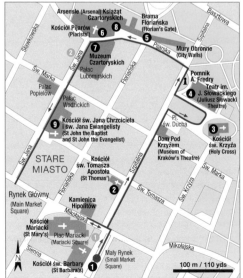

Piarists' Church ceiling

Czartoryski Museum

The Arsenal

Meanwhile, the Czartoryski's Ancient Art Gallery, with examples of works from Greece, Etruria, Egypt and Rome, has reopened in the **Arsenal ❽** across the street from the main building (Galerii Sztuki Starożytnej w Arsenale Książąt Czartoryskich; ul Pijarska 8; www.muzeum.krakow.pl; Tue–Sun 10am–4pm; charge).

Opposite the museum is the **Polskie Jadło Compendium Culinarium**, a good choice for a long lunch, see ❷.

CHURCH OF THE STS JOHN

Head south along ul. św Jana. On the left, just before ul. św Tomasza, is the **Church of St John the Baptist and St John the Evangelist ❾** (Kościół św Jana Chrzciciela i św Jana Ewangelisty). While the foundations and crypt of the original 12th-century Romanesque church have survived, the predominantly Baroque characteristics derive from the 17th century. The black and gold side altars form a vivid contrast with the otherwise plain white interiors.

Adjacent to the main altar is a painting of *Matka Bożej od Wykupu Niewolników* (Holy Mary Mother of God, of Releasing Prisoners of War) also known as *Matka Boska Wolności* (Holy Mary Mother of God of Liberty), which was donated by Duke Stanisław Radziwiłł – who acquired it in Spain – in about 1577. Since the early 17th century, this painting has been associated with those Polish prisoners of war who were 'miraculously' freed after being sentenced to death by the Ottomans. The handcuffs of one such liberated prisoner still hang by the painting. King Jan III Sobieski, who, after defeating the Turks at the Battle of Vienna, prayed here in 1684 as a token of gratitude.

Continue along ul. św Jana to return to Main Market Square.

Food and Drink

❶ ALBO TAK CAFÉ

Mały Rynek 4; tel: 012 421 11 05; www.albotak.pl; Mon–Sat 10am–midnight, Sun noon–11pm; €

A young crowd of locals, expats and visitors has made this little place the best location on Small Market Square. The prices help – it is one of the cheapest places in the Old Town – as does the quirky decor and friendly staff. A good place for a coffee or beer; little food served though.

❷ POLSKIE JADŁO COMPENDIUM CULINARIUM

Ul. św Jana 30; tel: 012 433 98 25; daily noon–11pm; €€€

It's the oom-pah-pah atmosphere as opposed to the food that keeps people coming back here. There's a band – usually from a remote mountain village – almost nightly and a variety of game dishes are served in huge portions.

WAWEL

Before there was Krakow, there was Wawel, and this route takes in both the royal castle and the cathedral, including the sumptuously furnished apartments that were once home to Poland's kings. Arrive early – to see everything, you are best advised to spend a whole day here.

DISTANCE: N/A – the tour is spent in the grounds of Wawel
TIME: A full day
START: Wawel Castle
END: Dragon's Cave
POINTS TO NOTE: Access Wawel via a route leading from Podzamcze to Herbowa Gate; the ticket office is to your right on the square. Or enter via Bernadyńska Gate, at the top of the path opposite the end of ul. Grodzka: a visitors' centre is on the left. Buy cathedral tickets at the office opposite the cathedral entrance. Visitor numbers on the hill are restricted and entry to some sights is by timed ticket only. The ticket offices close 75 mins before the exhibitions; to reserve tel: 012 422 51 55 ext. 291. Collect reserved tickets at the office near the entrance to the arcaded courtyard at least 20 mins before the reserved time. The hill is open longer than the buildings, from Apr–Sept 6am–8pm, Nov–Mar 6am–5pm. See www.wawel.krakow.pl.

Wawel Castle and **Cathedral** sit on a 228m- (750ft-) high limestone hill overlooking the Wisła (Vistula) River. For food options while you're here, Kawiarnia pod Basztą next to the visitors' centre offers hot meals, snacks, and drinks, and has two café terraces for fine days. Słodki Wawel Café sells drinks and ice-creams. Both are reasonably priced but can get crowded. You could also bring a packed lunch to eat in the gardens or try one of the restaurants down the hill, such as Smak Ukrainski on ul. Kanonicza, see ➊.

Background

Wawel Hill was established as the royal residence in 1038 when King Kazimierz Odnowiciel (Casimir the Restorer) transplanted the capital from Gniezno to Krakow and began building a royal home here. Under King Kazimierz Wielki (Casimir the Great, 1333–70) this evolved into a Gothic castle complex with defensive walls and towers that was subsequently extended by King Władysław Jagiełło (1386–1434).

Wawel Hill lit up at night

Fire and reconstruction

The castle was ravaged by fire in 1499, but some of its Gothic elements, such as the Kurza Stopa (Hen's Foot Tower), survived and were incorporated into a larger castle built by King Zygmunt Stary in 1506–35. He wanted a palatial residence and he certainly succeeded in creating one. The castle's perfectly proportioned; its three-storey, arcaded courtyard is one of Europe's finest examples of Renaissance architecture. The designs were initiated by the Italian architect Francisco the Florentine and, in 1516, continued by another Italian architect, Bartolomeo Berrecci. The castle was finished in 1536, but subsequent fires meant refurbishment was required; in 1595, Giovanni Trevano introduced the early Baroque elements and two additional towers.

Invasion of the Swedes

Warsaw was declared the capital of Poland in 1596, and King Zygmunt III Waza (1587–1632) transferred the royal residence to Warsaw's Royal Castle in 1609. Though Wawel's importance was diminishing, it remained the site of the royal treasury and continued to hold coronations and royal funerals.

Wawel was ravaged and looted during the Swedish invasion of 1665–7, and the castle torched by Swedish soldiers in 1702. In the 1780s, King Stanisław August Poniatowski commissioned the Italian architect Dominik Merlini to oversee the refurbishments, introducing neoclassical elements. The partitions of Poland at the end of the 18th century saw the Prussians, then the Austrians, loot the royal treasury. Austria turned the castle into a military barracks.

20th-century Wawel

It wasn't until 1905 that Austrian troops left the castle and renovation work could begin. Work was still in progress, when the Germans invaded in 1939. The main body of the castle had opened as a museum when Poland

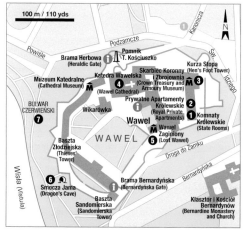

Sigismund's Chapel is crowned by a gilded dome

regained independence in 1918. A large amount of the castle's treasures was shipped to Canada during the first few days of the invasion, thus denying the Nazis some handsome booty. The castle and cathedral became a museum again in 1945.

WAWEL CASTLE

From the main Wawel courtyard, walk past the cathedral and through the alleyway leading into a second courtyard, known as the Castle Courtyard. In the far, southeastern corner is the entrance to the **State Rooms and Royal Private Apartments** (Reprezentacyjne Komnaty i Prywatne Apartamenty Królewskie; Apr–Oct Tue–Fri 9.30am–5pm, Sat 10am–5pm, Sun 10am–4pm, Nov–Mar Tue–Sat 9.30am–4pm, Sun 10am–4pm, Royal Private Apartments closed Sun, both closed Mon all year; charge, State Rooms free Sun Nov–Mar; admission to Royal Private Apartments in groups of up to 10, tours only, fee includes a guide).

State Rooms
The castle's **State Rooms** ❶ (Komnaty Królewskie), spread over the ground and second floors, may be viewed without a guide, though it is best to follow the 'suggested' route. This takes you through the former **Governor's Suite** on the ground floor, the highlight of which is the reception room, whose original 16th-century fur-

niture and décor remain. The Baroque tapestries that adorn the walls are of particular note. Climbing the **Deputies' Staircase** to the second floor, you will emerge in the Tournament Hall, which has impressive Italian furniture brought from Siena.

The adjoining **Audience Hall** (Sala Poselska) is perhaps the most famous in the castle. Also known as **Hall under the Heads** (Sala Pod Głowami), it is notable for its ceiling adorned with 30 sculpted heads of kings, knights, burghers and allegorical and mythical figures; the 30 heads are all that remain of 194 originally commissioned by Zygmunt Stary.

Walk back past the staircase to the **Hall under the Eagle** (Sala Pod Orłem), showcasing royal portraits such as Rubens's *Elizabeth of Bourbon* (1629). The **Hall Under the Birds** (Sala Pod Ptakami) is where King Zygmunt III Waza received foreign delegations – note the royal crest on a 16th-century wall-hanging and on the stone portal.

Next door is the castle's largest hall, the **Senators' Hall** (Sala Senatorska), which served as the home of the Senate. It displays an impressive tapestry, one of a magnificent collection of wall-hangings commissioned in the mid-16th century by King Zygmunt Stary (and later by his son, King Zygmunt August) and displayed throughout the castle. Of the original 360, only 142 survived the Nazis.

Stained-glass window in the cathedral

Royal Private Apartments

On leaving the Senators' Hall, you need to return to the ground floor to pick up the guided tour of the sumptuous **Royal Private Apartments** ❷ (Prywatne Apartamenty Królewskie), which are in fact located on the first floor. The tour passes through various Renaissance and Baroque apartments, including the **King's Suite**, of which the highlight is his office, featuring rich 16th-century stucco decoration. Two dark, windowless rooms lead off from here, in the so-called **Hen's Foot Tower** (Kurza Stopa): their purpose is unknown, but they may well have been prisons.

The **Guest Bedroom** features the oldest tapestry in the castle, from the 15th century, and a late Renaissance English-style fireplace. The Italian paintings are all part of the magnificent **Lanckoroński Collection**, once held in the Lanckoroński Palace in Vienna (the Lanckorońskis were wealthy Cracovians who moved to Vienna after Poland's partition in 1795). After the fall of Communism in Poland, the Countess Karolina Lanckorońska donated the collection to Wawel's museum authorities.

Treasury and armoury

As you leave the Royal Private Apartments, the entrance to the **Crown Treasury and Armoury Museum** ❸ (Skarbiec Koronny i Zbrojownia; Apr–Oct Mon 9.30am–1pm, Tue–Fri 9.30am–5pm, Sat–Sun 10am–5pm, Nov–Mar Tue–Sat 9.30am–4pm, closed Mon–

Sun; charge, free Mon Apr–Oct) is on your right, on the same side of the courtyard, housed in a Gothic part of the castle. The 13th-century *szczerbiec* ('jagged sword'), used at Polish coronations from 1320, is one of the most important exhibits of coronation regalia and medieval sacral art.

The **Museum of Oriental Art** (Sztuka Wschodu; Apr–Oct Tue–Fri 9.30am–5pm, Sat–Sun 10am–5pm, Nov–Mar Tue–Sat entrance only at 11am and 2pm; charge) brings together Turkish pavilions, armour, rugs and porcelain, some of which was taken as booty after the Battle of Vienna.

WAWEL CATHEDRAL

As the scene of royal coronations, weddings, funerals and state occasions, **Wawel Cathedral** ❹ (Katedra Wawelska; www.katedra-wawelska.pl; Apr–Sept Mon–Sat 9am–5pm, Sun 12.30pm–5pm, Oct–Mar Mon–Sat 9am–4pm Sun 12.30pm–4pm, Cathedral Museum closed Sun; Cathedral free, charge Sigismund's Bell, Royal Tombs, Cathedral Museum) is Poland's most important church. A set of prehistoric bones by the entrance portal has hung here for centuries. Local superstition holds that the bones are those of a dragon that terrorised the city from its cave beneath the castle; only while the bones remain in place will the cathedral be safe. The scientific verdict links them to prehistoric mammals.

Locals contest a game of chess

The interior

The cathedral was built on the site of two Romanesque churches. It blends Gothic, Renaissance and Baroque, but also has some Seccessionist windows by Józef Mehoffer. Entering through the main entrance, ahead of you is the Baroque main altar, which dates from the mid-17th century and features an emotive painting of the Crucifixion.

Taking a clockwise route around the cathedral you will pass a total of 18 impressive side chapels dating from the 14th to 18th centuries. The most spectacular one, **Sigismund's Chapel** (Kaplica Zygmuntowska, 1519–33), the fourth on the right, was designed by Santi Gucci, Padovano and Berreccio. It is regarded as one of the finest examples of Renaissance sacral art in Europe. Crowned by a gilded dome, using 50kg (110lbs) of gold leaf, the chapel is the Jagiellonian dynasty's mausoleum.

Royal tombs

At the head of the church is the **Stefan Batory Chapel**, opposite which are the **royal tombs**. The earliest is the sarcophagus of King Władysław Łokietek (1333). The highly ornate tomb of St Stanisław, Poland's patron saint, with bas-reliefs depicting his life, dates from 1671 and was sculpted in Gdańsk. The bishop was murdered in 1079 on the orders of King Bolesław the Bold, who didn't appreciate the bishop's criticisms of his immoral lifestyle.

Opposite, in a Baroque altar from 1745, is the **Cross with the Black Christ** (Gothic Krzyż z Czarnym Chrystusem). It was brought to Poland by Queen Jadwiga, who left her native Hungary in 1384 aged 10. She was canonised by Pope John Paul II in 1997 for her endless charitable work and for promoting Catholicism in Poland.

The crypt

More royal tombs, as well as those of renowned Poles such as the poets Adam Mickiewicz and Juliusz Słowacki, Tadeusz Kościuszko (who led the 1794 uprising), and the 20th-century statesman Marshal Józef Piłsudski, can be seen in the **crypt**, accessed via an entrance to the left of the main altar. More recently, President Lech Kaczynski was controversially interred here after the 2010 plane crash that killed many of Poland's political and military elite.

The first section, known as St Leonard's Crypt, is a prime example of Romanesque style. This is where the newly ordained Fr Karol Wojtyła (subsequently Pope John Paul II) celebrated his first Mass on 2 November 1946. As Bishop of Krakow he presided over Wawel Cathedral for 10 years.

Sigismund's Bell

The largest bell in Poland, run only on special occasions, **Sigismund's Bell** (Dzwon Zygmunta), in the cathedral's **Sigismund's Tower** (Wieża Zygmuntowska; same times as cathedral; charge), was

Inside Wawel Castle   *Sigismund's Bell*

cast in 1520 and weighs almost 13 tonnes. Climbing the tower's staircase is tough, but worthwhile. According to legend, touching the bell's clapper with your left hand will grant you a wish.

Cathedral Museum

Opposite the cathedral entrance is the **Cathedral Museum** (Muzeum Katedralne; Mon–Sat 9am–5pm; charge), set up by the late John Paul II when he was Archbishop of Krakow. Here we can see 12th- to 18th-century sacral art and relics.

LOST WAWEL

Across the garden from the cathedral, housed within the former royal kitchens and coach house, **Lost Wawel** ❺ (Wawel Zaginiony; Apr–Oct Mon 9.30am–1pm, Tue–Fri 9.30am–5pm, Sat–Sun 10am–5pm, Nov–Mar Tue–Sat 9.30am–4pm, Sun 10am–4pm, closed Mon; charge, free Mon Apr–Oct Sun Nov–Mar) includes archaeological and architectural remains, such as Gothic tiles and the rotunda of the Church of the Blessed Virgin Mary, one of the earliest buildings on Wawel Hill.

SANDOMIERSKA TOWER

For a fine view to the south, climb the 137 steps of the Sandomierska Tower (Baszta Sandomierksa; daily Apr, Sept–Oct 10am–5pm, May–June 10am–6pm, July–Aug 10am–7pm,

closed winter; charge), built in 1460 by Kazimir IV Jagiellon.

DRAGON'S CAVE

At the far end of the castle grounds are steps leading down to the **Dragon's Cave** ❻ (Smocza Jama; daily late Apr, Sept–Oct 10am–5pm, May–June 10am–6pm, July–Aug 10am–7pm, Nov–Mar closed; charge), thought to be one of several under Wawel Hill and once said to be home to a fearsome dragon. At the exit, Bronisław Chromy's dragon sculpture breathes real flames.

BY THE RIVER

Between Wawel and the Wisła is a small strip of parkland known as **Bulwar Czerwieński** ❼, which is popular in the summer with the locals as a place to relax in the sun or take boat trips. In the high season, boats moored by the river sell food and drink.

The Star of David in the Tempel Synagogue

KAZIMIERZ

Explore Kazimierz, the rapidly changing historic Jewish district of Krakow, taking in an array of synagogues, a number of Jewish museums and cultural centres, and a host of cafés and restaurants.

DISTANCE: 2km (1.25 miles)
TIME: A full day
START: Tempel Synagogue
END: New Jewish Cemetery
POINTS TO NOTE: To reach Kazimierz from Main Market Square walk along ul. Grodzka, then follow ul. Stradomska until ul. Krakowska then turn left into ul. Miodowa. Many trams serve this route: nos.8 or 13 go to the centre. Kazimierz is as lively during the evening – if not more so – as it is during the day. For the full Kazimierz experience, you can stay in one of the area's hostels; more are opening all the time and a few offer a full kosher package.

Kazimierz was founded as a town in its own right just outside Krakow by King Kazimierz Wielki (Casimir the Great), who gave the town his own name, in 1335. Although Kazimierz is known as a centre of Jewish life, it was not totally so – the district has several historic Roman Catholic churches. Kazimierz has had Jewish connections since 1495, the time of King Jan Olbracht's expulsion of Krakow's Jewish population. Many settled in Kazimierz, where they were soon joined by other persecuted Jews from across Europe.

Flourishing community

Commerce thrived and, by the 16th century, the town's Jewish community was one of the most prominent in Europe. Indeed the renowned Talmudic scholar and philosopher Rabbi Moses Isserles (known as Remuh) founded his academy here. Kazimierz became a walled town, complete with gateways, town hall and market place in the early 17th century. Only at the end of the 18th century, when this part of Poland was annexed by the Austro-Hungarian Empire, was Kazimierz incorporated into Krakow.

The Holocaust

When Germany invaded Poland in September 1939, about 70,000 Jews lived in Kazimierz, most of whom were soon 'resettled' in other parts of the country. In 1941 the Nazis established a Jewish ghetto in Podgórze, a separate dis-

The ornate interior of Tempel Synagogue

trict of Krakow, into which they herded Kazimierz's remaining 20,000 Jews. Yet unlike so many of the Continent's centres of Jewish life, Kazimierz survived.

TEMPEL SYNAGOGUE

At the junction of ul. Podbrzezie and ul. Miodowa you will see the Reform (rather than Orthodox) Jewish congregation's **Tempel Synagogue ❶** (ul. Miodowa 24; Sun–Fri 10am–4pm; charge). Constructed in 1862, it was extended on both sides in 1924. Of the few houses of Jewish prayer in Kazimierz that sur-

vived the Nazi regime virtually intact, this was the newest.

Beautiful interior

Whereas the facade combines neo-Romanesque with Moorish influences, the interior blends ornate stucco work, red-and-gold intricately painted walls and a set of four circular stained-glass windows. Above highly gilded galleries on both sides, the beautiful ceiling is decorated with gold stars on a light-blue background. An exhibition area includes photographs and architectural drawings of all the synagogues in Kazimierz,

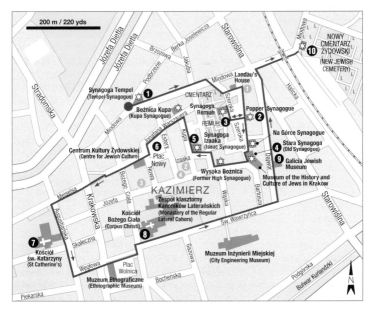

Remuh Synagogue dates back to 1558

together with historical details.

Across the road, beyond a courtyard, you can see the rear of the 17th-century **Kupa Synagogue**. The front of this building is on ul. Warszauera.

UL. SZEROKA

Continue past ul. Jakuba and turn right into **ul. Szeroka** (Wide Street) and you will be in what was once the centre of Jewish life and commerce in Kazimierz. There was a time when this quiet neighbourhood was the most prestigious residential street inhabited by the wealthiest Jews. Restoration work has preserved its Jewish character. You'll hear wandering troubadours play nostalgic tunes in the Jewish cafés and restaurants.

The substantial **Landau House** at no. 2 was built as a manor house in the 16th century. Overlooking a small green, it now houses the Jarden bookshop, which stocks a good range of guidebooks.

Dating from the 16th century, the **Klezmer-Hois** (no. 6; see ❶), a café and restaurant with rooms, occupies a building that used to house the *mikveh* (ritual baths).

Approached through a courtyard at no. 16, the **Popper Synagogue** ❷ was founded in 1620 by Wolf Popper, a wealthy merchant and financier known as Bocian ('Stork'), because of his habit of standing on one leg. Originally decorated and furnished in a lavish style, it was destroyed by the Nazis. It is now used as a cultural centre.

REMUH SYNAGOGUE

Crossing to the opposite side of the wide street, you will find that the smallest synagogue in Kazimierz, **Remuh** ❸ (ul. Szeroka 40; Sun–Fri 9am–4pm; charge) is not merely a historic monument – it remains the centre of the neighbourhood's Jewish life and has an active, albeit small, congregation. Remuh, which dates from 1558, was the town's second synagogue, and was originally known as the 'New Synagogue'. The founder, Israel ben Joseph, was a merchant and banker to King Zygmunt II August, and the father of the renowned philosopher and rabbi Moses Isserles, known as Remuh (1525–72).

Approach the synagogue via a small, irregular courtyard and you'll see a harmonious blend of architectural genres. The current appearance dates from the major refurbishment of the 1820s and the post-war reconstruction. A rectangular, single-aisle hall is overlooked by a women's gallery. The stone collection box by the entrance to the prayer room dates from the 16th century, while the altar features a plaque commemorating the spot where Remuh prayed, and there are Renaissance stone portals and Secessionist doors.

Renaissance cemetery

The synagogue has its own Wailing Wall in the adjoining **cemetery**, on the ul. Szeroka side. This was built with fragments of Nazi-desecrated tombstones

The Remuh's Wailing Wall   *Gravestones in the synagogue's cemetery*

that were too small to be reconstructed. One of two Renaissance Jewish cemeteries in Europe (the other is in Prague), it was used from 1551 until the early 19th century. Some 700 gravestones, including ornate Renaissance and Baroque examples, fill 4.5 hectares (11 acres). If you're ready for a coffee or lunch break, try **Szara Kazimierz** beside the synagogue at no. 39 (see page 121) or **Ariel** restaurant at no. 18 (see page 119).

OLD SYNAGOGUE

At the southern end of the street is Poland's oldest surviving synagogue, **Old Synagogue ❹** (Stara Synagoga; ul. Szeroka 24; www.mhk.pl; Apr–Oct Mon 10am–2pm, Tue–Sun 9am–5pm, Nov–Mar Mon 10am–2pm, Tue–Thu and Sat-Sun 9am–4pm, Fri 10am–5pm; charge, Mon free), home to the **Museum of the History and Culture of Jews in Krakow**. Dating from the early 15th century, this building was partly modelled on synagogues in Prague, Regensburg and Worms, which explains the Gothic facade. It was extended in the 16th century, when the architect Matteo Gucci of Florence introduced the synagogue's Renaissance elements. In the following century, a women's prayer room and a meeting hall for the Jewish community authorities were established on the first floor. The synagogue remained the centre of Jewish worship in Kazimierz until the Nazi invasion. The Nazis used it as a warehouse before destroying the interiors and roof. It wasn't until several years after the war that the ruins were reconstructed. The synagogue reopened as a museum in 1959.

Museum of the History and Culture of Jews in Krakow

The museum's extensive collection provides such good explanations of the Jewish faith, its history and culture that, even if you have little prior knowledge, it is easy to understand the significance of each exhibit. Many of the religious items have been collected from other synagogues. The gallery on the first floor features 19th- and early 20th-century views of Kazimierz.

A monument in front of the museum marks the site where 30 Polish men and boys were executed by Nazis in 1943. A plaque also marks the spot where Polish revolutionary Tadeusz Kościuszko rallied the Jews to join his fight for Polish independence in 1794.

TWO FORMER SYNAGOGUES

To the left of the Old Synagogue is the former **Na Górce Synagogue**. Though the name's literal translation is 'Synagogue on the Hill', it actually means 'Upper Synagogue', signifying that the prayer hall was on the first floor (the ground floor housed a *mikveh*). This synagogue was known for its connection with the Kabbalist rabbi Nathan Spira.

High Synagogue wall inscription

High Synagogue

Leave ul. Szeroka by the southwestern corner and head along ul. Józefa where you will find the former **High Synagogue** (Bożnica Wysoka; no. 38) on the right, dating from the mid-16th century and restored after its destruction by the Nazis in 1939. The facade features a Renaissance portal and four elegant buttresses. As at Na Górce, the prayer hall was on the first floor. The building now houses a branch of the city's conservation department and a bookshop.

Lunch options

There is no shortage of restaurants in Kazimierz, so you may have already seen one you'd like to try. **Warsztat** in ul. Izaaka has many fans, see ❷; other good choices are **Pub Stajnia** through a famous archway at ul. Józefa 12, see ❸, or **Singer** café, see ❹.

Kazimierz's revival

From the end of World War II until Poland's return to democracy in 1989, Kazimierz was one of the most deprived and dangerous areas of Krakow. Since 1989, however, Polish Jews who had emigrated have been free to return to the area either to reclaim confiscated property or simply to invest, and have driven a remarkable turnaround in fortunes. Cheap property prices at the beginning of the 1990s encouraged young Polish entrepreneurs to set up shop here, as bar and restaurant owners and shopkeepers. Students – attracted by cheap rents – soon followed.

Add the lively cultural scene – which grew up around the resurrected Centre for Jewish Culture – and the area was already blooming long before Steven Spielberg really put it on the map in the film *Schindler's List*. (The courtyard at ul. Józefa 12, leading into Pub Stajnia, features in the early part of the film.) While property prices are now among the highest in Krakow, the area is still popular with students and has retained its bohemian character.

ISAAC SYNAGOGUE

Just after the High Synagogue turn right into ul. Jakuba, then left into ul. Izaaka. Ul. Izaaka was named after Isaac Jakubowicz, one of 17th-century Kazimierz's wealthiest merchants and moneylenders and founder of the Isaac Synagogue. Built by Giovanni Battista Trevano in 1644, the **Isaac Synagogue** ❺ (ul. Kupa 18; Sun–Thu 9am–7pm, Fri 9am–3pm; charge) is the largest in Kazimierz, and was, by contrast to the minimalist interior you see today, also the most lavishly furnished.

Ravaged by the Nazis, the building served as a sculptor's workshop after the war, and it wasn't until 1983 that renovation work began. Nevertheless, the Baroque prayer hall retains a distinctive beauty and features fragments of recently uncovered 17th-century wall murals together with some stucco decoration by Giovanni Falconi. On the

The Isaac Synagogue   *Shady outdoor café*

east wall is a stone altar tabernacle; the women's gallery features an elegant arcade of Tuscan columns. In another part of the synagogue, adjoining a photographic exhibition of pre-war life entitled 'The Memory of Polish Jews', you can see films tracing the history of Jewish life in Krakow and Kazimierz.

NEW SQUARE

Turn right from the synagogue, on to ul. Kupa, and walk towards the **Kupa Synagogue** (Bożnica Kupa) at the end of the street. Turn left on to ul. Warszauera and continue for 100m/yds into **Plac Nowy** ❻ (New Square). The central small, circular building, today occupied by fast-food stalls, was once a Jewish slaughterhouse. Though its bric-a-brac and fruit and vegetable stalls remain, the square has been revived by an influx of cafés and bars.

CENTRE FOR JEWISH CULTURE

Cross over to the Centre for Jewish Culture (**Centrum Kultury Żydowskiej**; Judaica Foundation, ul. Meiselsa 17; www.judaica.pl; Mon–Fri 10am–8pm, Sat–Sun 10am–2pm, also open in the evenings for special events and concerts). Established in 1993 and concealed behind the 1886 period facade of a former prayer house, the centre's motto, L'dor v'dor (Hebrew for 'from generation to generation'), emphasises its commitment to Jewish culture and conti-

nuity after the Holocaust. The centre runs a full programme of cultural and international events and also incorporates a workshop, art gallery, bookshop and café.

ST CATHERINE'S CHURCH

Continue along ul. Meiselsa, crossing u. Krakowska, and turn right into ul. Augustiańska for a simple snack at Kuchnia U Doroty (see page 120), or continue left to St Catherine's Church ❼ (**Kościół św Katarzyny**; ul. Augustiańska 7). This prime example of Gothic architecture was founded by King Kazimierz the Great in 1349. There is a legend it was a form of penance for sentencing Fr Marcin Baryczka to death by drowning in the River Vistula. This was a classic case of shooting the messenger: the priest had committed the heinous crime of conveying the bishop's disapproval of the king's dalliances with various mistresses.

The church's interiors include Baroque details, such as the impressive altar. The cloisters of the adjoining Augustinian monastery feature remarkable frescoes from the 14th and 15th centuries. An altar dedicated to Matka Boska Pocieszenia (Our Lady the Consoler) was one of the most important sites in Poland's cult of the Virgin Mary.

ETHNOGRAPHIC MUSEUM

Continue along ul. Augustiańska and turn left into ul. Węglowa, where you will shortly reach **Plac Wolnica**, the

Ethnographic Museum paintings

former main marketplace of Kazimierz and once an important trading point on the salt route. The square is overlooked by the **Ethnographic Museum** (Muzeum Etnograficzne; Pl. Wolnica 1; www.etnomuzeum.eu; entrance to second part of museum in Dom Esterki, ul. Krakowska 46; Tue–Wed, Fri–Sat 11am–7pm, Thur 11am–9pm; Sun 11am–3pm; charge, Sun free). This is housed in a splendid early 15th-century building that served as the town hall of Kazimierz until 1800 and which was continually extended and restyled until the mid-19th century.

The museum features an interesting collection of folk arts and crafts gathered from various villages in the regions of Krakow, Podhale and Silesia. They include paintings, sculpture and costumes, as well as naive sacred art and Christian exhibits such as Easter eggs painted with rustic motifs. Recreated interiors featuring period furniture are redolent of traditional village homes. The collection extends beyond the Polish boundaries, with rarities such as late 19th-century Siberian fur coats and folk costumes from Belarus and the Ukraine.

CHURCH OF CORPUS CHRISTI

Leave the square by the northeastern corner, where you will soon see the **Church of Corpus Christi ❽** (Kościół Bożego Ciała; ul. Bożego Ciała 26). It is another of Krakow's beautiful Gothic churches founded by Casimir the Great. The reason behind the establishment of the church at this particular location is interesting: apparently it was here that fleeing thieves abandoned a monstrance containing the holy Eucharist which they had stolen from All Saints' Church (Kościół Wszystkich Świętych), which no longer exists.

Building began in 1340, but Corpus Christi wasn't completed until the beginning of the 15th century, when it became the parish church for Roman Catholics living in Kazimierz. King Władysław Jagiełło invited the canons of the Lateran Order to supervise the church – their residences can still be seen across the courtyard by the entrance. Among the Gothic, Renaissance and Baroque elements of this ornate but dignified church is the Renaissance tombstone of Bartolomeo Bereccio, who designed the Zygmunt Chapel and the exquisite Gothic stained-glass windows in Wawel Cathedral. The gilded main altar includes a painting of the Nativity by Tommaso Dolabella, while the ornamental pulpit takes the form of a boat.

GALICIA JEWISH MUSEUM

Turn right along ul. św Wawrzynca, pass the City Engineering Museum (Museum Inżynierii Miejskiej) and turn left into ul. Dajwór, where you will find the **Galicia Jewish Museum ❾** (Galicja Żydowskie Muzeum; www.galiciajewishmuseum.

Traditional moccasins   *Photographs in the Galicia Jewish Museum*

org; daily 10am–6pm; charge). Supported by charitable donations, this museum was set up to present Jewish history and culture in a different way and performs a valuable educational role. At its heart is a permanent exhibition of photographs, Traces of Memory, taken by its founder, the late Chris Schwartz, but it also runs a very full programme of concerts, lectures and workshops. Its bookshop and café are well worth a visit, too.

NEW JEWISH CEMETERY

At the end of ul. Dajwór turn right, crossing ul. Starowiślna, into ul. Miodowa, and walk beyond the viaduct to reach the **New Jewish Cemetery** ❿ (Nowy Cmentarz Żydowski; Sun–Fri 9am–5pm or sunset) at no. 55. The cemetery, established at the beginning of the 19th century to replace the Remuh burial ground, contains the graves of many renowned Jews.

Food and Drink

❶ KLEZMER HOIS

Ul. Szeroka 6; tel: 012 411 12 45; www.klezmer.pl; daily 8am–11pm; €€€
The hotel café has a bourgeois air – oil paintings, roses on each table and comfortable sofas make for a very pleasant scene. The restaurant manages to be more formal and more stylishly bohemian at the same time. Its klezmer bands ensure a lively evening. Jewish and Polish dishes include excellent chłodnik (cold beetroot soup with sour cream and dill) and walnut cake.

❷ WARSZTAT

Ul. Izaaka 3; tel: 012 430 14 51; www.restauracjawarsztat.pl: Mon–Thu 9am–10pm, Fri-Sat 9am–2am, Sun 9am–1am; €€€
A long pizza and pasta menu and lots of soups and salads, mean you can lunch here inexpensively, but you can treat yourself with a special, such as chicken fillet with wild mushrooms or even steak in truffle sauce.

❸ PUB STAJNIA

Ul. Józefa 12; tel: 012 423 72 02; www.pubstajnia.pl; Sun–Thu 11am–1am, Fri–Sat 11am–3am; €€€
This long-established Kazimierz haunt has both a garden and a cosy fireplace. The menu features a mix of Italian and Polish favourites. A relaxed place to eat in the daytime, this pub becomes a cheerful nightspot for an older crowd after dark.

❹ SINGER

Ul. Estery 20/ul. Izaaka 1 tel: 012 292 06 22; daily 9am–last guest; €€
You won't be in Kazimierz long before you realise that lace and old sewing machines are the default décor. As the café that started this craze, Singer has a lot to answer for, but it's still a popular place for coffee and cake or something stronger.

National Museum paintings

NATIONAL MUSEUM

This route is a visit to the National Museum, the city's largest and most comprehensive, housed in a rather stark 1930s' Modernist edifice, and the surrounding area west of the historic centre. For a pleasant picnic lunch, take a detour to Krakow's largest park, Jordan.

DISTANCE: 1km (0.6 mile) not including detour to Jordan Park
TIME: A half day
START: National Museum
END: Capuchin Church
POINTS TO NOTE: To reach the museum from the Old Town, take tram no. 20 three stops from Barbican (a short walk north of Main Market Square). To walk directly to the museum from Main Market Square will take around 15 mins.

NATIONAL MUSEUM

The **National Museum 1** (Muzeum Narodowe; al 3 Maja 1; www.muzeum. krakow.pl; Tue–Fri 10am–6pm, Sun 10am–4pm; charge, Sun and permanent collection free) is one of the highlights of the city, housing a fabulous collection of historic works of art.

To the right as you enter the building, is the Arms and Uniforms Gallery, showcasing some 1,600 military objects from the 10th to the 20th centuries.

Completely renovated in 2009 with videos and interactive exhibits, it includes poignant memorabilia of the 18th- and 19th-century rebellions against partition and military decorations as well as medals from World War II.

Gallery of Decorative Arts

Spanning the centuries from the early Middle Ages to 20th century Art Nouveau, the arts and crafts on display on the first floor detail Krakow's history as the country's centre of fine art. Here you'll find silver and gold, sacred art, clocks, furniture, fashion, glass, and a collection of ceramics that includes Polish and European decorative tiles, faience and porcelain, with examples by Meissen and Sèvres.

20th-century Polish Art and Sculpture

Through more than 400 words the galleries on the second floor tell the story of the development of Polish art from the Młoda Polska (Young Poland, a movement that inspired Stanisław Wyspiański, Wojciech Weiss, Józef Mehoffer) through the avant-garde Krakow

Nothing Inside!, J. Sawicka

Morning mist in Jordan Park

Group of the early 20th century, to modern and contemporary art by the likes of the Expressionist Stanisław Witkiewicz.

JORDAN PARK

A pleasant detour from the route can be made by exiting the museum through the main entrance, turning right along al. Krasińskiego, right again along al. Focha and then bearing right along al. 3 Maja: in a couple of minutes you arrive at the large **Jordan Park** (Park dr H. Jordana), named after a 19th-century Cracovian doctor, and the vast **Błonia** meadow. It's one of the few green spots in the city where picnicking is tolerated, and Jordan will be popular with kids, who can take a boat ride around the artificial lake. Football supporters might want to take a look at the stadium of Wisła, Krakow's leading team, at the western end of the park. They will have already passed the new stadium of Cracovia, Poland's oldest team, across the Błonia meadow from the park.

UL. MARSZAŁA PIŁSUDSKIEGO

From the entrance of the National Museum, take a right (passing the Wyspiański monument), then turn left at the main crossroads on to **ul. Marszała Józefa Piłsudskiego** (named after the statesman and inter-war commander). The main street of the Nowy Świat (New World) district, it is home to some elegant architecture, much of which dates

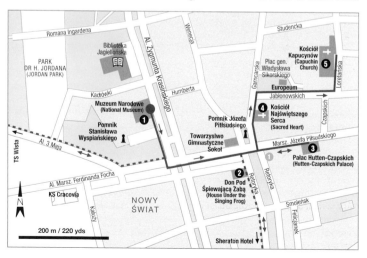

House Under the Singing Frog

from the early 19th century. You'll find Towarzystwo Gimnastyczne 'Sokół' at no. 27, the gymnasium of an organisation founded in 1867 to promote fitness. It was a cover for the military training of Krakow's youth during the period of partitions. Opened in 1889, it's the city's oldest gym.

On the corner of ul. Piłsudskiego and ul. Retoryka is the **House Under the Singing Frog ❷** (Dom Pod Śpiewającą Żabą). Designed by Teodor Talowski, it is a prime example of the neighbourhood's 'historic revival' architecture. Neighbouring buildings at ul. Piłsudskiego 30, 32, 34 and 36 are eclectic Secessionism. Turning into ul. Retoryka, numbers 3, 7 and 9 are Talowski creations from 1887–91. Avoid even looking at the bland modern blocks on the other side of the road. For a break at this stage, take a detour to the end of ul. Retoryka, to ul. Powiśle, where The Sheraton is home to restaurants and bars including **Someplace Else** and **The Olive** (see page 106).

Hutten-Czapskich Palace

Further along ul. Piłsudskiego at no. 12 is the late 19th-century neo-Renaissance **Hutten-Czapskich Palace ❸** (Pałac Hutten-Czapskich; Tue–Sat 10am–6pm, Sun 10am–4pm, charge), bequeathed by the Hutten-Czapski family to the National Museum in 1902. It houses a fine collection of historic coins and notes.

At no. 16 is a neoclassical building where the novelist Henryk Sienkiewicz,

who won the Nobel Prize for Literature in 1905, often stayed. For a pitstop, retrace your steps to **Pub Kuranty**, see ❶.

TWO CHURCHES

Head back west along ul. Piłsudskiego, and turn right into ul. Garncarska where the **Church of the Sacred Heart ❹** (Kościół Najświętszego Serca) at no. 26 presents a typical combination of a neo-Gothic facade and neo-Renaissance and Secessionist interiors.

Turn right into ul. Jabłonowskich, passing Plac Sikorskiego, home to the National Museum's Europeum permanent exhibition of European art, and then left into ul. Loretańska. The **Capuchin Church ❺** (Kościół Kapucynów), at no. 11, was commissioned by the Capuchin Order late in the 17th century in accordance with its vow of poverty – hence its pronounced air of modesty.

Food and Drink

❶ PUB KURANTY

Ul. Piłsudskiego 24; tel: 012 430 90 00; www.kuranty.ostoyapalace.pl; daily noon–midnight, kitchen closes 10pm; €€€
This renovated 19th-century palace has a cellar bar-restaurant serving a mix of Polish and Italian dishes. The traditionally styled room is cosy in winter, though in summer the lack of daylight is a drawback.

St Anne's Church interior

HISTORICAL COLLEGES AND IMPOSING CHURCHES

Visit some of the Jagiellonian University's historic colleges, including Collegium Maius and Collegium Nowodworskiego, and two of the city's most imposing churches, the Franciscan and the Dominican.

DISTANCE: 1km (0.6 mile)
TIME: A (long) half day
START: St Anne's Church
END: Main Market Square
POINTS TO NOTE: St Anne's Church is easy to reach from the Main Market Square: walk 250m/yds along ul. Szewska, then take a left turn through the small park.

ST ANNE'S CHURCH

For a flamboyant example of the Baroque style, begin at **St Anne's Church** ❶ (Kościół św Anny; ul. św Anny 11; daily 9am–noon, 4–6pm). Modelled loosely on Rome's Church of St Andrew della Valle by Tylman of Gameren, who designed many of Poland's most beautiful Baroque structures, St Anne's was built as the university church between 1689 and 1703. The earliest reference to a church on this site dates from 1381. Its successor was a Gothic church funded by King Władysław Jagiełło. That was in turn

demolished in 1689, having become too small for the congregation.

The dome of St Anne's Church was painted by the Italians Carlo and Innocente Monti and represents the ultimate victory of Catholicism, depicted as Christianity's one true faith. Sculptures (including one of St Anne herself) and magnificent stucco designs featuring fruit and floral motifs are the work of the Italian Baldassare Fontana.

COLLEGIUM NOWODWORSKIEGO

Across the road is **Collegium Nowodworskiego** ❷ (Nowodworski College; ul. św Anny 12), which was founded as a grammar school in 1586 by Bartłomiej Nowodworski, one of the king's private secretaries. The present building, the university's Collegium Medicum, complete with arcaded courtyard, dates from 1643 and is the oldest Polish college still in use. The actual building isn't open to the public, but there is permanent access from the street to the courtyard. For those feeling peckish the

Basilica of St Francis mosaic

super **Chimera Salad Bar** is a 50m/yds detour from here further along ul. św Anny at no. 3, see ①. A more substantial meal can be had at **Trattoria Soprano** (see page 117).

COLLEGIUM MAIUS

Pick up the walk on ul. Jagiellońska. Now a museum, **Collegium Maius** ❸ (Great College; www.maius.uj.edu.pl; Apr–Oct Mon–Sat 10am–5.20pm, Sun closed, Nov–Mar Mon, Wed–Sat 10am–2.20pm, Tue until 3.20pm, Sun closed; charge, entry by guided visit only, times vary for English language tours, advance booking recommended) at no. 15 was Poland's first university college. Entrance to the courtyard is free whenever the college is open, but admission to the museum is only as part of a guided tour.

Collegium Maius clock

Five times a day (9am, 11am, 1pm, 3pm, 5pm), the great clock above the entrance to the museum plays the university tune *Gaudeamus Igitur* and a procession of figures from the history of Krakow appears. Though these were carved in the 1950s, the clock is ancient: a 'clock of great size' was documented as having been repaired at the university in 1465 and there are records of at least four restorations since. If you do not catch it on your walk, it is a short walk from the Main Market Square.

The college itself originated in Wawel Castle in 1364. In 1400 King Władysław Jagiełło bought a house on what is now Ul. Jagiellońska from a wealthy merchant family called Pęcherz to serve as the seat of the college, then known as Academia Cracoviensis. The house was soon extended, and neighbouring houses were acquired. These buildings burnt down in the late 15th century, and a purpose-built college with an elegant Gothic facade took their place. Completed in 1492, when it became known as Collegium Maius, it included the arcaded cloister, from which 'professors' staircases' lead up to the professorial chambers on the first and second floors.

Professors' Dining Room

The professors' common room, the treasury, assembly hall and library were built in 1507–19 in Gothic style. The library features a beautifully painted skyscape on the vaulted ceiling, as well as historic portraits and various rare tomes – it became the university library in 1860. The former professors' dining room has distinctive Gdańsk cupboards and an extensive collection of gold and silver tableware.

Copernicus Room

The **Mikołaj Kopernik Room** commemorates the life of the renowned astronomer Nicholas Copernicus (1473-1543), who studied here in 1491–5, before going on to study in Bologna, Padua

Collegium Maius door detail   *Astrolabe in the Copernicus Room*

and Rome. His then-revolutionary theory that the sun and not the earth was the centre of the universe, and that the earth and planets revolved around the sun, was set forth in *De Revolutionibus Orbium Coelestium*, which was published in 1530.

Sections of the original manuscript can be seen in the Copernicus Room, together with a collection of historic portraits, astrolabes and other early astronomical instruments. A 1510 golden globe, one of the first to show the New World, bears the inscription America, *terra noviter reperta* (America, a newly discovered land).

BASILICA OF ST FRANCIS

Turn left into ul. Gołębia, where you can make for the poetic **Café Gołębia 3**, for a break, see ②. Then turn right into ul. Bracka, leading to the **Basilica of St Francis of Assisi ④** (Bazylika św Franciszka z Asyżu; entrance from ul. Franciszkańska 1, or Plac Wszystkich Swiętych 5; Mon–Sat 10am–3pm, Sun 1–3pm). Striking in its imposing beauty, this church was founded for the Franciscan Order, which arrived in Krakow in 1237. Designed in the form of a Greek cross, and built in Gothic style between 1252 and 1269, it was extended dur-

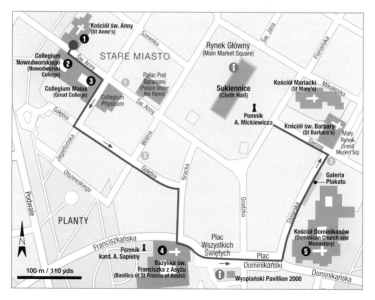

Collegium Maius assembly hall

ing the 15th century thanks to King Bolesław Wstydliwy (Boleslaus the Bashful), who is buried here.

Tadeusz Popiel Mosaic

The Great Fire of Krakow in 1850 destroyed some historic features and resulted in further rebuilding in a neo-Gothic style. But the church has retained historic elements, such as the Gothic galleries and fragments of wall paintings in the adjoining Franciscan monastery. By the Baroque altar, the apse features a Tadeusz Popiel mosaic depicting St Francis of Assisi. The Chapel of Our Lady the Sorrowful has a 15th-century painting of the Madonna, and fine polychrome.

Mehoffer and Wyspiański

The church showcases the work of two of the country's greatest Secessionist artists. The paintings representing the Stations of the Cross are by Józef Mehoffer, while the stunning polychromy on the walls and vaulted ceilings was designed by Stanisław Wyspiański.

The effect of this intense combination of Gothic and floral motifs with Secessionist elements is dazzling, though it can take time to adjust your eyes to the sombre lighting. Paradoxically, the semi-darkness heightens the beauty of the stained-glass windows, also designed by Wyspiański. Stand in the main nave and look up at the most important of these windows, over the main entrance. Completed in 1900, it is an astonishing depiction of the Creation.

Nicholas Copernicus

Polish astronomer Nicholas Copernicus (1473–1543) was the first person to formulate a scientifically based heliocentric cosmology that displaced the earth from the centre of the universe. Born in Toruń in central Poland to wealthy parents, Copernicus was by profession an economist, mathematician and diplomat, often carrying out delicate business for the Polish King Sigismund I. Astronomy was for Copernicus very much a hobby pursued only when time allowed, making his achievements all the more incredible. It was his work above anything else that made the Jagiellonian University one of the most respected seats of learning in the whole of Renaissance Europe.

DOMINICAN CHURCH

Another extraordinary ecclesiastical centre is just across the square, past the Wyspiański Pavillion 2000 (Plac Wszystkich Świętych 2; tel 012 616 18 86; daily 9am–5pm), an official tourist information centre where you can see more stained glass by Wyspiański. The Basilica of the Holy Trinity, commonly known as the **Dominican**

The Dominican Church

The Madonna in the Chapel

Church and Monastery ❺ (Kosciół Dominikanów; ul. Stolarska 12; daily 9.30am–4.30pm, closed to tourists on Sun), is as austere as the Franciscan church.

The church originated in 1222, when the Dominicans reached Poland. The first, Romanesque, church, destroyed by the Tartars in 1241, was greatly extended during the 15th century, when Renaissance elements were added.

The **Chapel of St Dominic** is one of the most beautiful examples of Renaissance art in Poland, while the Rococo **Chapel of Our Lady of the Rosary**, which dates from 1685, contains a painting of the Madonna copied from Our Lady of the Rosary in Rome's Basilica of Santa Maria Maggiore.

You can also admire the cloisters located in the adjoining Dominican Monastery, where a large number of the city's most illustrious residents were laid to rest.

UL. STOLARSKA

Ul. Stolarska, which runs up to the edge of Mały Rynek from ul. Dominiskańska, was named after the carpenters who once plied their trade in workshops here. A great little café at no. 6, **Pierwszy Lokal**, see ❸, serves big pots of steaming tea and delicious cakes for tired tourists. A wooden arcade on the right-hand side of the street (nos 8–10) features various specialist shops. The grand buildings on the other side of the road house the French, German and American consulates.

At the end of ul. Stolarska turn left towards the Main Market Square.

Food and Drink

❶ CHIMERA SALAD BAR
Ul. św. Anny 3; tel: 012 292 12 12; www.chimera.com.pl; Mon–Sat 9.30am–10pm, Sun 10am–10pm; €€
This self-service cellar salad bar with garden is at the end of a passage off the street. Don't confuse it with the U Chimera restaurant close by. Choose from the likes of herring salad or turkey stuffed with liver and raisins. Lovely fresh food.

❷ CAFÉ GOŁĘBIA 3
Ul. Gołębia 3; tel: 012 430 24 19; Mon–Sat 9am–11pm, Sun 10am–11pm; €
This cosy bohemian café's student patrons sit at wobbly tables and take advantage of the WiFi. The rather tasty cakes and coffee are worth the visit.

❸ PIERWSZY LOKAL
Ul. Stolarska 6/1; tel: 012 431 24 41; Mon–Sat 6.30am–1am, Sun 10am–1am; €€
Opening early for office workers who take breakfast and coffee here, this place serves as a typical Krakow café during the day before transforming into a hip and trendy bar as the sun goes down.

Elegant Grodzka Street

TWO HISTORIC THOROUGHFARES

Ul. Grodzka combines imposing town houses, august institutions and stunning churches; the adjoining ul. Kanoniczna, one of the city's oldest and most exquisite streets, boasts several museums.

DISTANCE: 1km (0.6 mile)
TIME: A (long) half day
START: Ul. Grodzka
END: Church of the Missionary Priests
POINTS TO NOTE: Ul. Grodzka was the southern part of the Royal Route, which took kings from Florian's Gate to Wawel. Pick it up at the southeastern corner of Main Market Square. Note that this is a long route and involves walking along often very crowded, narrow streets. A good idea is to have an early lunch before heading off.

UL. GRODZKA

The long, beautiful **ul. Grodzka** ❶, leading from the Main Market Square to Wawel Castle and believed to be the site of the first Cracovian settlement outside of Wawel, is a bustling partly pedestrianised, thoroughfare, with a mix of restaurants, cafés and bars, shops and galleries. Its origins pre-date Krakow's town charter: it was probably established as a main street in the 9th century. Ul. Grodzka was traditionally known as Droga Solna (the Salt Road) because it heads off towards the Wieliczka and Bochnia salt mines. Though ul. Grodzka no longer plays host to royal processions, each year on Corpus Christi (Boże Ciało in Polish), a major parade of locals in traditional dress makes its way from Wawel to the Main Market Square.

Historic facades

Among the most attractive houses, **House Under the Lion** (Dom Pod Lwem) at no. 32 has a 14th-century stone lion carved above the portal. **Pod Aniołami** (Under the Angels) at no. 35 is a delightful, folksy Polish restaurant and café with an atmospheric vaulted cellar and a charming patio garden, see ❶.

At no. 38, **House Under the Elephants** (Dom Pod Elefanty) is thought to have been the residence and premises of Bonifacio Cantelli, a 17th-century royal apothecary. The exotic animals on the facade formed an apothecary's sign — not to be confused with the golden elephant at no. 11 Plac Wszyst-

House Under the Elephants   *The 12 Apostles, Church of Sts Peter and Paul*

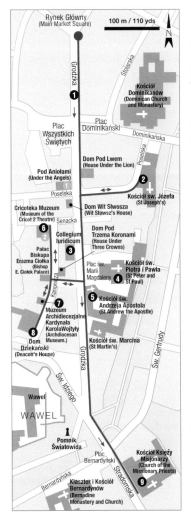

kich Świętych. There is another excellent Polish restaurant at no. 40, **Miod Malina** (see page 116). Across the road, **Wit Stwosz's** (Veit Stoss') **House** (Dom Wit Słwosza) at nos 39–41 was the residence of the master carver of St Mary's altar from 1478 to 1492.

Turn left into ul. Poselska and at no. 21 you'll find the Baroque **St Joseph's Church** ❷ (Kościół św Józefa) and the adjoining Bernardine Convent.

Back on ul. Grodzka at no. 53 is the Jagiellonian University's **Collegium Iuridicum** ❸, which dates from the 14th century, and was restyled and extended in the 16th century. Originally the law school, this college now houses the university's history of art faculty. Beyond an attractive Baroque portal, you will see an arcaded courtyard.

Church of St Peter and St Paul

Opposite, at no. 54, the **Church of St Peter and St Paul** ❹ (Kościół św. Piotra i św. Pawła) is a splendid example of Baroque architecture approached through a walled courtyard set with 12 late Baroque sculptures of the Apostles. Those you see today are copies of the originals carved in the early 18th century. The courtyard is an aesthetic overture to a magnificent Baroque facade designed by Zygmunt III Waza's architect Giovanni Battista Trevano. Commissioned by the Jesuits, the design was modelled on the Jesuit church of Il Gesù in Rome, following the form of a Latin cross. The impres-

Pope John Paul II

sive stucco work, at its finest in the apse, where it depicts the lives of St Peter and St Paul (1619–33), is by Giovanni Battista Falconi. This church also features a model of Foucault's pendulum, which demonstrates the rotation of the Earth.

Church of St Andrew the Apostle
Equally fine is the **Church of St Andrew the Apostle** ❺ (Kościół św Andrzeja Apostoła), at no. 56. An early Romanesque church with a pair of elegant towers, it was founded at the end of the 11th century and withstood the Tartar siege of 1241 thanks to its 1.5-m- (5-ft-) thick walls. The exquisite Baroque interior is on a far smaller scale than the facade suggests. Wall paintings by Balthazar Fontana and 18th-century stucco work are set between a vaulted ceiling decorated with putti and acanthus leaves, and a stunning 18th-century marble floor. The gilded altar is matched by a gilded limewood pulpit in the form of a fishing boat. Adjoining the church is the 14th-century Order of St Claire (Klasztor Klarysek), established in Poland in 1245 at the behest of Duke Leszek Biały.

STREET OF THE CANONS

Opposite the church of Sts Peter and Paul, a statue of Piotr Skarga by Czesław Dźwigaj dominates pl. św. Marii Magdaleny, which sometimes hosts art exhibitions and otherwise is a favourite with skateboarders. It leads to the tranquil **ul. Kanonicza** (Street of the Canons). This lane lined with ornate houses and palaces was named after the clergymen from Wawel Castle who lived here in the 15th and 16th centuries.

Buildings of note
At the northern end of the street, no. 1 has an impressive Baroque portal. The **Cricoteka Museum** ❻ (no. 5; www. cricoteka.pl; Mon, Wed–Fri 10am–2pm Tue 2–6pm; charge) is home to the Centre for the Documentation of the Art of Tadeusz Kantor, which traces the rise of the avant-garde Cricot 2 Theatre, and is a good example of Gothic architecture.

Contrast this with the Renaissance facade of the **House Under Three Crowns** (Dom Pod Trzema Koronami) at no. 7, home to La Campana Italian restaurant (see page 113). Look hard above the plain portal of no. 6 to see the wall painting of the Madonna of Częchostowa. At no. 18 a Renaissance doorway leadings to a 14th-century building housing the John Paul II Institute.

At no. 17, the first of a trio of key ecclesiastical buildings, the 16th-century **Bishop Erazm Ciołek Palace** (Pałac Biskupa Erazma Ciołka; www.muzeum. krakow.pl; Tue–Sat 10am–6pm, Sun 10am–4pm, Mon closed; charge, Sun permanent exhibitions and courtyard free) has a restful courtyard, but it is worth exploring the museum here dedicated to the Art of Old Poland between

Ul. Kanonicza   *Church of the Missionary Priests exterior*

the 12th and 18th centuries, with some beautiful and simple Madonnas, while on the ground floor you will find a separate exhibition featuring many ancient icons, devoted to Orthodox Art of the Old Polish Republic.

Archdiocesan Museum

The building at no. 19 is the **Archdiocesan Museum ❼** (Muzeum Archidiecezjalne Kardynała Karola Wojtyły; Wed–Fri 10am–4pm, Sat–Sun 10am–3pm; charge). It houses a fine collection of sacred art, but many will be more interested in the replica of Pope John Paul II's study between 1952 and 1958, when he became bishop of Krakow. He then moved next door to no. 21.

This, the **Deacon's House ❽** (Dom Dziekański) is a gem in a street rich in fine architecture. Originally late 14th-century, it features a spectacular portal and an arcaded cloister added in the 16th century. The 14th-century house at no. 25 was once that of the medieval chronicler Jan Długosz, and later the studio of Stanisław Wyspiański's father, a sculptor.

For a well-earned coffee break, try **U Literatów** (Among the Literati, a café at ul. Kanonicz 1, see ❷).

Church of the Missionary Priests

Return to ul. Grodzka, head south in the direction of the Wawel and you'll find ul. Stradomska, a busy, gritty street with the beautiful **Church of the Missionary Priests ❾** (Kościół Księży Misjonarzy) at no. 4.

The Church of the Missionary Priests was established in France by St Vincent de Paul in 1624. This particular church was built between 1719 and 1728 by Kacper Bażanka in a late Baroque style. The facade was inspired by Bernini's Sant' Andrea al Quirinale Church in Rome, while the stylised interiors were based on Borromini's work.

Food and Drink

❶ POD ANIOŁAMI

Ul. Grodzka 35; tel: 012 421 39 99; www. podaniolami.pl; daily 1pm–midnight; €€€
One of Krakow's most popular restaurants, decorated with 'folk chic' touches and with open cooking ranges and a lovely patio garden under a glass roof at the rear. The grilled oscypek (smoked ewe's cheese, a speciality of the Tatras) is a highlight.

❷ U LITERATÓW

Ul. Kanonicza 7; tel: 012 421 86 66; daily 10am–10pm; €€
A firm favourite with Krakow's literary set, this café is a reminder of the days when cafés meant coffee, cigarettes and discussion. There's alfresco seating in a cobbled courtyard garden, while the fin-de-siècle town house decoration, including a piano and comfy sofas, creates a charming, elegant time capsule inside.

Monument to the Battle of Grunwald

MATEJKO SQUARE

Explore the north of the city around Matejko Square (Plac Matejki), a showpiece of late 19th- and early 20th-century styles and home to some of Krakow's most notable historic buildings and ancient churches.

> **DISTANCE:** 1km (0.6 mile)
> **TIME:** A half day
> **START:** Matejko Square
> **END:** Church of the Nuns of the Visitation
> **POINTS TO NOTE:** Leave the historic centre along ul. Floriańska, through St Florian's Gate and head past the Barbican to the square.

ON THE SQUARE

The central feature of **Plac Matejki** is the **Monument to the Battle of Grunwald ❶** (Pomnik Grunwaldzki). This commemorates one of the greatest battles in medieval Europe, fought in 1410 by up to 60,000 soldiers. The victory of the Polish and Lithuanian army over the Teutonic Knights effectively ended the Knights' dominance of Poland. Erected to mark the battle's 500th anniversary in 1910, the original monument was destroyed by the Nazis and reconstructed in 1976. In front of it is a memorial to the Unknown Solider. Opposite is the Polish restaurant **Jarema**, see ❶.

Academy of Fine Arts

The square's architecture is eclectic. Its largest building is the opulent **Polish State Railways Headquarters**

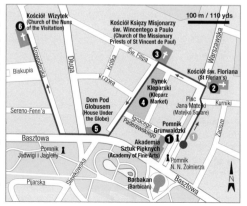

Church of the Nuns detail   *House Under the Globe*

at no. 12 (closed to the public). Next to it at no. 13, the **Academy of Fine Arts** (Akademia Sztuk Pięknych; tel: 012 299 20 00; www.asp.krakow.pl; open by prior appointment only) has a facade designed in 1879 by Maciej Moraczewski featuring a bust of Poland's great 19th-century painter, Jan Matejko, above the main entrance. Matejko was instrumental in establishing the academy before becoming its first rector.

St Florian's Church

In the northeastern corner of the square is **St Florian's Church** ❷ (Kościół św Floriana), traditionally the beginning of the 'Royal Way', the route by which kings of Poland entered the city to be crowned at Wawel. The church was built to house the remains of St Florian (one of Krakow's patron saints), which were brought to Poland in 1184 at the instigation of King Kazimierz Sprawiedliwy (Casimir the Just). Consecrated in 1226, the Romanesque church was rebuilt several times over the centuries after Tartar sackings and fires.

AROUND THE SQUARE

Head west along św Filipa. On your right at no. 19 is the **Church of the Missionary Priests of St Vincent de Paul** ❸ (Kościół Księży Misjonarzy św Wincentego a Paulo). Built in 1876–7, it was extended (in 1911–12) to include a chapel with a figure of Our Lady of Lourdes. Both this and a painting of the Crucifixion are said to have miraculous powers.

House Under the Globe

Head south past **Kleparz Market** ❹ (Rynek Kleparski; Mon–Sat 7am–4pm), and turn right into ul. Basztowa: ahead of you is the 1906 **House Under the Globe** ❺ (Dom Pod Globusem) at the junction with ul. Długa. Designed (and still used) as commercial premises, it is a geometric, uniform example of Secessionism but has none of the flamboyance of the city's other buildings of this period.

Church of the Nuns of the Visitation

Continue along ul. Basztowa, turn right into ul. Krowoderska and you'll find the 17th-century Baroque **Church of the Nuns of the Visitation** ❻ (Kościół Wizytek) at no. 16. The church is under the patronage of St Francis de Sales, whose mission was to provide religious education for the young.

Food and Drink

① JAREMA

Pl. Matejki 5; tel: 012 429 36 69; www.jarema.pl; daily noon–1am; €€€
Behind a charming facade, Eastern Polish cuisine dominates the menu here, including dishes from Lithuania (once a Polish province).

A superfluity of nuns near St Nicholas' Church

CHURCHES OF EASTERN KRAKOW

Simply by strolling along ul. Mikołaja Kopernika (Nicholas Copernicus Street) you can see a remarkable number of beautiful and historic churches; en route you can take a break at the Botanical Gardens.

DISTANCE: 1.5km (1 mile)
TIME: A half day
START: St Nicholas' Church
END: Celestat Museum
POINTS TO NOTE: From Main Market Square walk east towards the Westerplatte to pick up ul. Mikołaja Kopernika (several trams also run along this way). Eat before setting off and bring something to drink with you, as there are no restaurants and bars en route. Don't dismiss the Botanical Gardens in the winter – the greenhouses can provide pleasant respite from the cold.

Wesola, the name of this part of the city, may be slowly becoming forgotten, even by locals, but the suburb is still noteworthy. Bordered by leafy trees, ul. Mikołaja Kopernika is a majestic promenade. Lined with grand houses, well-kept gardens and quiet courtyards, it was once where the city's elite lived; today it is home to some of Krakow's most revered academic institutions.

ST NICHOLAS' CHURCH

One of the city's oldest churches is **St Nicholas' Church** ❶ (Kościół św Mikołaja; open during services only) at no. 9. The earliest reference to this church dates from the 12th century, before it was rebuilt in a Romanesque style in 1229. In 1456 it was taken over by the Benedictine Order. For all the Gothic restyling of the 15th century, and the addition of Baroque elements between 1677 and 1682, a fair number of original Romanesque sections have survived. The courtyard's medieval sculpture, known as the 'Lamp of the Dead', resembles a miniature church tower.

SOCIETY OF PHYSICIANS

Opposite the church, on the left-hand side of ul. Radziłłowska, is Krakow's **Society of Physicians** ❷ (Gmach Towarzystwa Lekarskiego; no. 14; www.tlk.cm-uj.krakow.pl; Tue and Fri 10am–2pm, Sat 4pm–8pm). It was built in 1904 and made sublime by its interiors, many designed by Stanisław

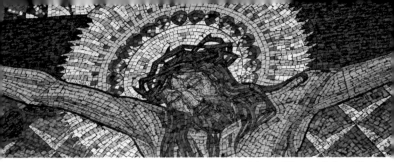

Mosaic of Christ in the Jesuit Church

Wyspiański. Its stained-glass window featuring Apollo is one of Krakow's hidden treasures.

JESUIT CHURCH

Back on ul. Kopernika, continue under the railway bridge and look to your left. At no. 26 the **Jesuit Church** ❸ (Bazylika Najświętszego Serca Pana Jezusa, Jezuitów; daily 9am–noon and during services) is an extraordinary example of *fin-de-siècle* Modernism, not just in terms of style, but also in scale – it's 52m (170ft) long, 19m (62ft) wide and has a 68m (223ft) high tower. First established in 1868, it evolved from a much smaller chapel. In 1893 the Jesuits decided to turn the chapel into a church that would be Poland's centre of the cult of the Sacred Heart. It was designed by the celebrated architect Franciszek Mączyński and completed in 1921.

A number of the country's finest artists and craftsmen were commissioned to work on the church. Note the entrance portal and integral sculptures by Ksawery Dunikowski. Particularly dazzling are Brother Wojciech Pieczonka's series of mosaics, and the magnificent *Hołd Narodu Polskiego Sercu Bożemu* (Homage of the Polish Nation to the Sacred Heart) designed by Piotr Stachiewicz and imported from Venice.

Bukowski murals

Vivid Secessionist murals with floral motifs by Jan Bukowski extend along a nave that's remarkable for its granite and marble pillars. The neo-Renaissance main altar, with a colonnade supporting statuary, and a mosaic extending along the apse, is highly unusual. A more recent addition is the Chapel of the Eternal Adoration of the Blessed Sacrament, completed in 1960, when the church was classified as a basilica.

CHURCH OF THE IMMACULATE CONCEPTION

Continue along ul. Kopernika; hospital buildings line both sides of the road. On the right at no. 19, set behind a walled forecourt, is the mid-17th-century Baroque **Church of the Immacu-**

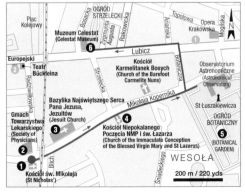

The Marksmen's mascot

late Conception of the Blessed Virgin Mary and St Lazarus ❹ (Kościół Niepokalanego Poczęcia NMP i św Łazarza; daily 8am–4pm). Since the 18th century, this has been the official church of the city's main hospital. Its most fascinating feature is a remarkable vaulted ceiling, painted a vivid blue. The adjacent monastery houses one of the wards of the University Hospital.

A little further along on the right at ul. Kopernika 44 is the Church of the Barefoot Carmelite Nuns (open only during services), a small convent church worth seeing for its oversized entrance, complete with Corinthian columns and elegant Baroque motifs. The convent of the Discalced Carmelite nuns connected to the church was the scene of the tragic history of the deranged nun Barbara Ubryk, who was imprisoned in her cell for over 20 years, until this particular 'skeleton' was released from the convent's 'cupboard' in 1869.

BOTANICAL GARDENS

At the end of the street, on the right at no. 27, are the **Botanical Gardens** ❺ (Ogród Botaniczny; www.ogrod.uj.edu.pl; daily mid-Apr–mid-Oct 9am–5pm, in winter only open during some exhibitions 10am–2pm; greenhouses 10am–4pm and full hours on Fri; charge). Established in 1783, they were Poland's first and among the earliest in Europe. Originally comprising 2.5 hectares (6 acres), the gardens were laid out as an English-style landscaped park in 1820. Some of the trees planted then remain in the arboretum. The gardens were extended to their current size of almost 10 hectares (25 acres) after World War II, and in the 1960s lots of tropical specimens and greenhouses were added.

The gardens are an adjunct of the university, which has always emphasised its educational aspect. Many botanists have learnt their craft here, and the grounds are punctuated by statues of the country's leading figures in the field. In addition to the arboretum, there are medicinal shrubs, Alpine plants (including specimens from the Carpathian Mountains, the Balkans, the Caucasus and the Alps), ponds, pools and lawns with ornamental borders. Two palm houses feature tropical and subtropical plants.

Museum

There's a small **museum** (Wed and Fri 10am–2pm, Sun 11am–3pm) in an attractive villa, although most exhibits are labelled in Polish only. Among the exhibits are plant specimens and old prints and maps that outline the garden's origins and evolution. One of the most notable exhibits displays 260 types of wood, culled from trees native to or cultivated in Poland.

MARKSMEN'S FRATERNITY

From the Botanical Gardens, head north along ul. Botaniczna and turn left into

Botanical Gardens   *Portraits of former kings of the Marksmen's Fraternity*

ul. Lubicz. As you do so, glance right along ul. Lubicz and you will see the contemporary Opera Krakowska building, opened in 2008. About 150m/yds along ul. Lubicz on the right is the restaurant **Trzy Kroki w Szaleństwo**, see ①. If you don't have the time to stay and eat right now, it's well worth making a reservation to sample this culinary experience another time.

Slightly further on is the **Celestat Museum** ❻ (Muzeum Celestat; ul. Lubicz 16; www.mhk.pl; closed for restoration until early 2015), situated on the right within a park. This unusual museum recounts the history of an organisation that has been integral to the city for centuries. Still extant, the Bractwo Kurkowe (literally 'Marksmen's Fraternity') was established in medieval times to teach civilians how to wield a rifle, should they need to defend the city.

The museum's collection includes portraits of champion marksmen and the club's mascot, the Silver Cockerel, which is a magnificent example of Renaissance art.

The brotherhood's Corpus Christi procession, with participants dressed in historic uniforms, is an annual highlight in the Old Town. Three weeks later, in a traditional ceremony on the Main Market Square, the outgoing king of the brotherhood ceremonially presents the Silver Cockerel to the new incumbent.

A short distance from the museum the Ogród Strzelecki (Rifle Marksmen's Garden) features monuments to two Polish kings: Jan III Sobieski (1629–96) and Zygmunt II August (1526–72), as well as to Pope John Paul II (1920–2005).

If you are hungry, walk a little further along ul. Lubicz, under the railway bridge and past the now redundant Teatr Buckleina (Buckleina Theatre), to the **Europejski Hotel**, whose **Kossakowka** restaurant serves decent Polish food, see ②.

Continue west on ul. Lubicz to reach the northeastern corner of the Planty.

Food and Drink

① TRZY KROKI W SZALEŃSTWO

Ul. Lubicz 28; tel. 012 430 04 38; http://trzykroki.pl; daily noon–10pm; €€€€
As the name translates, you are 'three steps into madness' as you sample this extraordinary European cuisine with elements of molecular cuisine. If you like experiments and pay attention to aesthetics, this is a place for you.

② KOSSAKOWKA

Ul. Lubicz 5; tel: 012 423 25 10; daily 6.30am–9.30pm; €€€
A pleasant enough place to refuel after completing this route, the Kossakowka restaurant at the Hotel Europejski is in itself something of a local historical treasure. Both the wine list and the menu have been updated and now have a modern slant, though there is little for vegetarians.

Nicholas Copernicus by Jan Matejko

MUSEUMS AND GALLERIES

A look at some of Krakow's more specialised museums and galleries, including the restored homes of Jan Matejko and Józef Mehoffer, modern art centres, the Pharmacy Museum and the Szołayski House Museum.

DISTANCE: 1.5km (1 mile)
TIME: A full day
START: Jan Matejko Museum
END: Józef Mehoffer House
POINTS TO NOTE: Pick up this route halfway along ul. Floriańska, a short walk from either Main Market Square or Florian's Gate. The time it takes to complete will depend greatly on how much time is spent in each museum: to do each museum properly a full day will be required, though by speed-viewing the museums a half day may prove sufficient. Note that most museums mentioned are closed Mondays. It's worth double-checking opening times on the individual museum websites before you set out, just in case of any late changes.

By any standards, Krakow is well served by museums. These range from the vast National Museum (see page 50) to a series of fascinating mini-museums designed to document specific themes, historical eras and celebrated artists.

JAN MATEJKO MUSEUM

For much of the 19th century, ul. Floriańska was the city's busiest street. Now closed to all but very limited traffic, it was the first street in Krakow to get a tram-line (1881), which ran from the railway station to Main Market Square. You can take a coffee on this street at the historic **Jama Michalika** café at no. 45, see ❶, then make your way a couple of doors down to the **Jan Matejko Museum** ❶ (Dom Jana Matejki; www.muzeum.krakow.pl; Tue–Sat 10am–6pm, Sun 10am–4pm; charge, Sun permanent exhibition free). First opened to the public in 1896, this is Poland's oldest biographical museum. Generally considered the greatest artist in the country's history, Matejko (1838–93) spent most of his life here. Matejko's oeuvre has a resonance that goes far beyond his considerable influence on his contemporaries. At a time when Poland was partitioned and thus didn't officially exist, his works were exhibited across Europe, becoming an important symbol of Polish identity.

Bust of Jan Matejko on the Palace of Art

Matejko's home

Though the museum preserves the atmosphere of a private home, with rooms furnished as they were when Matejko lived here, the restoration of the 15th century building before its re-opening uncovered some previously unseen wall paintings, and multimedia installations have been added that aim to give visitors a better insight into Matejko as man and artist – particularly in his third-floor studio, where the exhibition drawn from his historical paintings underlines his influence on how Poles thought of their past and themselves.

The grand first-floor salon overlooking ul. Floriańska contains neo-Renaissance furniture commissioned by the artist in Venice in 1878. There is a cabinet displaying some of his many awards, a beautifully painted skyscape ceiling in his bedroom and several self-portraits. Matejko's designs for the wall paintings in the Mariacki church are on display, as are his collections of antique military and architectural pieces, mementoes such as his palette, spectacles, chess set and walking stick, and a wooden horse complete with a ceremonial saddle on which his subjects could pose.

MUSEUM OF PHARMACY

You will find more than a simple history of chemists' shops at the **Museum of Pharmacy ❷**, a little further on down the street near the intersection with Św. Tomasza (Muzeum Farmacji; ul. Floriańska 25; www.muzeumfarmacji. pl; Tue noon–6pm, Wed–Sat 10am–2.30pm; charge). The museum occupies an elegant town house with a Renaissance portal, as well as Gothic and Baroque elements, and its decorative interiors and objects are worth seeing in their own right.

Cellars

In the museum's cellars you will find antique distillation equipment that might have been used by an alchemist. Indeed, legend has it that Dr Faust once studied at the Jagiellonian University, which is patron of this museum. The wine barrels on display

Pod Różą hotel sign

recall a time when, in the belief that alcohol promoted longevity and youthfulness, Polish apothecaries sold Italian and Hungarian wines – and, this being Poland, vodka – for medicinal purposes. Red wine was thought to be particularly beneficial.

First floor

The beautiful 19th-century stained-glass window on the first floor landing picturing a pestle, mortar and various herbs was taken from a chemist's shop in the city. The portrait gallery depicts various renowned apothecaries, while the reconstructed interiors include superb neo-Baroque and Biedermeier examples of 19th-century pharmacies. A remarkable collection of porcelain and glass urns, used to store ingredients such as preserved leeches, snakes and mandrakes, as well as less stomach-turning cures, is complemented by the calm calligraphy of handwritten prescriptions.

POD RÓŻĄ

Across the road, on the corner of Św. Tomasza, is the **Pod Różą** hotel ❸ (see page 104), one of the most historic in the city. Its fine rooms were once the stamping ground of Franz Liszt, among other notables, while in its oldest section you will now find the **Amarone** restaurant, a quiet and very good Italian eatery with an excellent wine list (see page 104).

PLAC SZCZEPAŃSKI

Walk a further 300m/yds along Św. Tomasza passing the Church of the Sts John (see page 35) on your right and the **Cherubino** restaurant, see ❷, on your left, and you arrive at **Plac Szczepański** ❹ (Szczepański Square), named after the Baroque Kościół św Szczepana (Church of St Stephen). Built by the Jesuits in the 13th century, the church was demolished at the end of the 18th century.

The square has now been completely renovated and what was formerly an eyesore and a permanent car park is now traffic free. The highlight is the fountain with numerous spurting jets, providing an attractive playground for children in the summer. The square has now become a popular meeting place and somewhere to relax and observe the surrounding buildings, which include a few attractions, including the **Morskie Oko** restaurant, see ❸, unmissable due to its huge wooden doors.

SZOŁAYSKY HOUSE

On the eastern side of the square (the entrance is round the corner on ul. Szczepańska) is the 17th-century **Szołaysky House** ❺ (Kamienica Szolayskich; www.muzeum.krakow.pl; Wed–Sat 10am–6pm, Sun 10am–4pm, Tue temporary exhibitions only; charge, Sun permanent exhibitions free), showcas-

Portrait by Wyspiański   *Inside Szołaysky House*

ing a substantial collection of work by Stanisław Wyspiański (1869–1907), one of Poland's foremost artists, poets and playwrights.

The collection

Following a complete renovation and modernisation of the building in 2012, it was decided to rename the former Stanisław Wyspiański Museum as **Szołaysky House.** There are new exhibition areas, temporary galleries, an information centre, shop, café and multi-purpose hall.

Born in Krakow, Wyspiański travelled but came back to make his artistic mark on every aspect of the city. He was a leading member of the Młoda Polska (Young Poland) Modernist movement, whose other members included Jósef Mehoffer, Olga Boznańska and Jacet Malczewski.

The collection includes pastel sketches and an iconic self-portrait, as well as works associated with the renowned Green Balloon Cabaret and other Polish Art Nouveau works. A gallery devoted to the illustrious poet Wisława Szymborska (1923–2012), and winner of the Nobel Prize for Literature in 1996, can be found on the ground floor. Temporary exhibitions are also regularly staged in the museum.

STARY TEATR

On the corner of the square, at the junction with ul. Jagiellońska, you'll come across **Stary Teatr** ❻ (Old Theatre, ul. Jagiełłońska 5; www.stary.pl;), the city's and Poland's oldest public theatre, established in 1799 by the renowned actor Mateusz Witkowski. In its mid-19th-century heyday, Helena Modrzejewska starred here before treading the boards in Warsaw and the US. The theatre was refashioned with wonderful Secessionist details in 1903 by the architects Franciszek Mączyński and Tadeusz Stryjeński, members of the Młoda Polska movement. After suffering several setbacks in the last century, it is beautifully

Stanisław Wyspiański

Polymath Stanisław Wyspiański (1869–1907) was a painter, poet, dramatist, theatre reformer, stage designer and typographer. His colourful and original paintings and stained-glass window designs for the Basilica of St Francis in 1898 signalled a major breakthrough for the Młoda Polska (Young Poland) art movement – an offshoot of Art Nouveau, or the Secession, that influenced art for two decades during the Austrian regency in Krakow. Alas, Wyspiański was as troubled as he was talented, and suffered from deep depression, often destroying recently completed work when fits would take hold. He died tragically young, of syphilis in 1907, at the age of 38. His legacy is as rich as his life was short.

Arts Bunker

restored and again a vibrant part of Krakow's cultural life.

Another example of Secessionism is the apartment at ul. Jagiellońska 2, built in 1909. A metalwork wreath crowns a stained-glass panel, with decorative balconies overlooking the square.

PALACE OF ART

Back on Plac Szczepański, two neighbouring buildings hold exhibitions of modern and contemporary art within very different settings. The aesthetic option is **Palace of Art** ❼ (Pałac Sztuki; pl. Szczepański 4; Mon–Fri 8.15am–6pm, Sat, Sun 10am–6pm; charge), a Secessionist building designed by Franciszek Mączyński, with a highly decorative frieze by symbolist painter Jacek Malczewski that includes busts of Matejko and Wyspiański. Apollo's huge radiant head tops the front of the building above the monumental entrance.

ARTS BUNKER

Built in 1968, the aptly named brutalist Arts Bunker (Bunkier Sztuki; Plac Szczepański 3a; www.bunkier.art.pl; Tue–Sun noon–8pm; charge) is the only intrusion of ugly, modern architecture in the city's historic centre. Owing to its grey concrete walls and bulky shape the unpopular structure was soon dubbed the 'bunker'. By the mid-1990s the contemptuous label was embraced by the exhibition hall's managers who turned their 'Bun-

ker of the Arts – The Contemporary Art Gallery' into a stronghold of the avant-garde. It has a thriving, varied and interesting programme of contemporary art exhibitions. Every third year the gallery serves as a main exhibition venue for the International Print Triennial, one of the world's biggest festivals of print arts. The Arts Bunker has an excellent bookshop, stocking reference books on contemporary Polish art and artists, plus prints, postcards and posters.

JÓZEF MEHOFFER HOUSE

Continue west across the Planty and along ul. Krupnicza, passing **Pod Norenami**, see ❹, to reach the **Józef Mehoffer House** ❽ (Dom Józefa Mehoffera; ul. Krupnicza 26; www.muzeum.krakow.pl; Tue–Sun 10am–4pm; charge, permanent exhibition free Sun). One of Poland's finest painters, Mehoffer (1869–1946) was a pupil of Matejko and, together with Stanisław Wyspiański, a pioneer of Modernism. In addition to landscapes, portraits and still life, he is known for his stained-glass windows.

Period interiors

The house is as notable for its stylish period interiors as for the abundance of Mehoffer's works. The artist bought the house in 1932 and most of it is furnished as it was in his day. The elegant dining room features charcoal portraits and architectural drawings of Krakow. In the library hangs a 1943 painting of the

Inside the J. Mehoffer House   *Stained-glass at the J. Mehoffer House*

garden he created (which can be visited Apr–Oct). The salon has a collection of family portraits, and there are two vast designs for stained-glass windows over the staircase. Secessionist furnishings include linen curtains embroidered with butterflies in Mehoffer's bedroom. By contrast, a Japanese room with scarlet walls and lacquered cabinets is a treas- ure trove of oriental objets d'art.

The restored garden, carefully repli- cating Mehoffer's original, is a delight- ful place to sit or stroll in summer, when the museum's Café Ważka (daily year- round 10am–9.30pm) puts out extra tables to serve snacks and drinks. Small-scale concerts are occasionally held in the garden.

Food and Drink

① JAMA MICHALIKA
Ul. Floriańska 45; tel: 012 422 15 61; www.jamamichalika.pl; Sun–Thu 9am–10pm, Fri–Sat 9am–11pm; €€
Open for over a century, this café was one of the main meeting places of the Młoda Polska (Young Poland) art movement. Almost all the decor is original, from the stained-glass windows to the artworks on the walls. Even the green balloon that gave its name to the Zielony Balonik cabaret is here.

② CHERUBINO
Ul. św Tomasza 15; tel: 012 429 40 07. www.cherubino.pl; Mon–Sat noon–midnight, Sun noon–11pm, reservations recommended at weekends; €€€
A Tuscan/Polish menu includes delicious favourites from each cuisine: antipasti, minestrone, risotto, *pierogi*. Lunch is served from 4pm. One dining room contains 18th- and 19th-century carriages and an ornate tiled stove, while the other is rustic-chic

Tuscan, with a wood-fired oven and a beamed ceiling.

③ MORSKIE OKO
Pl. Szczepański 8; tel: 012 431 24 23; www.morskieoko.krakow.pl; daily noon–midnight; €€€€
This restaurant has tried to save people the trouble of going to Zakopone by bringing the mountains to the people. Expect plenty of game, mountain stews and rich broths accompanied with lashings of smoked pork fat. Hunting trophies adorning the walls and raucous live folk music add to an enjoyable experience.

④ POD NORENAMI
Ul. Krupnicza 6; tel: 661 21 92 89; www.podnorenami.pl; Mon–Wed 7.30am–10pm, Thu–Fri 7.30am–11pm, Sat–Sun 10am–11pm; €€€
This Asian restaurant is tempting for all, but especially great for vegetarians and vegans. The attractive Japanese-style dining room is the perfect venue to taste sizzling stir-fries, mouth-watering tempura and a range of sushi.

Strolling in the Planty

GREEN KRAKOW

Escape the busy streets of the Old Town by circumnavigating Krakow's green belt. Follow the route of the old city walls, enjoy landscaped gardens and fine statuary, and explore quirky little side streets.

DISTANCE: 5km (3 miles)
TIME: A full day
START/END: Obelisk Floriana Straszewskiego
POINTS TO NOTE: Start by the subway leading to the Planty gardens from the main railway station. This is a long walk, but there are plenty of benches along the way, if you're in need of breaks.

The **Planty** is a series of individual landscaped gardens forming a green horseshoe around the city. Short on flowers, but big on shaded avenues, lawns, water features and monuments, the gardens were created during the 1820s when the Austrian authorities demolished the medieval city walls. Foundations of the walls can still be seen on this walk, along with plaques showing where bastions once stood.

NORTHERN PLANTY

On the left of the railway station subway is the **Obelisk Floriana Straszewsk-iego ❶**, honouring the 19th-century senator instrumental in planning the layout of the gardens.

Victims of Communist Aggression

From the obelisk, continue along the main footpath towards the Barbican, and you will pass a smaller monument dedicated to **Victims of Communist Aggression ❷** (Ofiarom Komunistycznej Prowokacji). Unveiled in 1936, it depicts trade union members clashing with the police. Removed by the Soviets, it was replaced in 1989.

Through the trees on the left is the flamboyant late 19th-century **Juliusz Słowacki Theatre** (Teatr im J Słowackiego, see page 122), one of Krakow's leading theatres, modelled on the Paris opera house.

Barbican

Walk another 150m/yds, passing Florian's Gate (see page 33) on your left, and you will arrive at the **Barbican ❸** (Barbakan; www.mhk.pl; daily April–Oct 10.30am–5pm, closed winter; charge). Having undergone a 10-year

Medieval Barbican   *Florian Straszewski, the Planty's founder*

restoration programme in the 1990s, the complex is one of Europe's biggest and best-preserved examples of medieval defensive architecture. King Jan Olbracht laid the foundation stone of this circular Gothic building that has walls up to 3.5m (11ft) wide at the base. It was surrounded by a deep moat more than 25m (82ft) wide, and linked to Florian's Gate by a bridge. You can walk around the battlements for fine views across the Planty and the interior courtyard.

Adjoining the final section of the city walls is the rear of the **City Arsenal** (Arsenał Miejski), now part of the Czartoryski Museum (see page 34).

Water features and monuments

Leaving the Barbican, you'll see one of the largest of the Planty's artificial lakes on your right, where silver birch trees, ponds and a fountain create an atmospheric setting for the 1886 statue of the poet **Bohdan Zalewski**.

Crossing ul. Sławkowska, a little further along you will see another 1886 monument marking the quincentenary of the **Polish-Lithuanian Commonwealth**. Walk another 200m/yds along the path that runs parallel to ul. Basztowa and you will see Alfred Daun's statue of his muse, **Lilla Weneda**. Daun created a series of statues for Krakow's parks in the early part of the 19th-century; his work can also be seen in Jordan Park (see page 51).

WESTERN PLANTY

Just to the southeast is the junction of ul. Pijarska and ul. św Marka. Proceed south along ul. Pijarska and turn right into ul. Reformacka, where on the right-hand side you'll find the **Church of St Kasimir ❹** (Kościół św Kazimierza), a 17th-century Baroque affair with fine Secessionist wall paintings.

Cross ul. św Tomasza to ul. Szczepańska and the corner of Szczepański Square. On the left is the Secessionist **Palace of Art** (Pałac Sztuki; see page 72); next is the 1960s **Arts Bunker** (Bunkier Sztuki). On the right Wacław Szymanowski's 1901 Secessionist monument to the Krakow painter **Artur Grottger** is set in a flower bed.

By the junction with ul. Szewska, the flower-painted **U Zalipianek Café** (Kawiarnia u Zalipianek) has an attractive open-air terrace with views of the Planty, see ❶.

Ul. Karmelicka and the Carmelite Church

Where the main Planty path crosses ul. Szewska, a worthwhile detour can be taken along **ul. Karmelicka**, to the right. The street once formed part of the route from Krakow to Łobzów (today a suburb of Krakow). It was for a time one of the finest streets in the city, and though its smart 19th-century town houses are today a little faded (and long since divided into smaller flats), they retain a latent elegance.

Alfred Daun's statue of his muse, Lilla Weneda

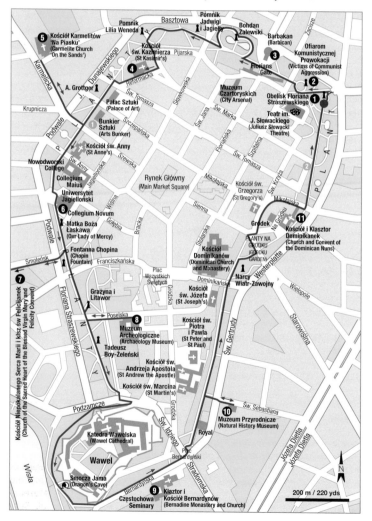

5 Kościół Karmelitów 'Na Piasku' (Carmelite Church 'On the Sands')

Pomnik Lilla Weneda

Basztowa

Pomnik Jadwigi i Jagiełły

Bohdan Zalewski

Barbakan (Barbican)

Ofiarom Komunistycznej Prowokacji (Victims of Communist Aggression)

Kościół św. Kazimierza (St Kasimir's)

Pijarska

4

3

Florians Gate

A. Grottger

Muzeum Czartoryskich (City Arsenal)

Obelisk Floriana Straszewskiego **1**

2

Pałac Sztuki (Palace of Art)

Św. Tomasza

Teatr im. J. Słowackiego (Juliusz Słowacki Theatre)

Krupnicza

Bunkier Sztuki (Arts Bunker)

Szczepańska

Kościół św. Anny (St Anne's)

Szewska

Św. Jana

Św. Marka

Floriańska

Św. Tomasza

Szpitalna

Św. Krzyża

2

Nowodworski College

Św. Anny

Collegium Maius

Rynek Główny (Main Market Square)

Mikołajska

Kościół św. Grzegorza (St Gregory's)

Uniwersytet Jagielloński

Jagiellońska

Wiślna

6 Collegium Novum

Matka Boża Łaskawa (Our Lady of Mercy)

Gołębia

Bracka

Sienna

Mikołajska

Na Gródku

11

Grodek

Kościół i Klasztor Dominikanek (Church and Convent of the Dominican Nuns)

Podwale

Fontanna Chopina (Chopin Fountain)

Franciszkańska

Stolarska

PLANTY NA GRÓDKU (GRÓDKU GARDEN)

Smoleńsk

Kościół Dominikanów (Dominican Church and Monastery)

Westerplatte

7

Grażyna i Litawor

Plac Wszystkich Świętych

Grodzka

Kościół św. Józefa (St Joseph's)

Dominikańska

Narcy Wiatr-Zawojny

Wielopole

Kościół Niepokalanego Serca Marii i ksz. św Felicjanek (Church of the Sacred Heart of the Blessed Virgin Mary and Felicity Convent)

Floriańska Straszewskiego

Poselska

8

Muzeum Archeologiczne (Archaeology Museum)

Tadeusz Boy-Żeleński

Kościół św. Piotra i Pawła (St Peter and St Paul)

Św. Gertrudy

Starowiślna

Kościół św. Andrzeja Apostoła (St Andrew the Apostle)

Podzamcze

Kościół św. Marcina (St Martin's)

Grodzka

Św. Sebastiana

10

Muzeum Przyrodnicze (Natural History Museum)

Józefa Dietla

Józefa Dietla

Wisła

Katedra Wawelska (Wawel Cathedral)

Wawel

Św. Józefa

Royal

Plac Bernardyński

Stradomska

N

Smocza Jama (Dragon's Cave)

Bernardyńska

9

Klasztor i Kościół Bernardynów (Bernardine Monastery and Church)

Częstochowa Seminary

200 m / 220 yds

The Secessionist-style Palace of Art

The Baroque **Carmelite Church and Convent 'On the Sands'** ❺ (Kościół Karmelitów 'Na Piasku') is found at no. 19, 300m/yds along ul. Karmelicka. The church is home to the 17th-century painting of *Our Lady of the Sands*, hence its name. According to legend, the Virgin Mary pointed out this site to an 11th-century Polish duke, who rubbed sand here into his body, curing his skin disease.

Collegium Novum

Picking up the main route again at ul. Szewska, pass St Anne's Church (see page 53) and Collegium Nowodworskiego (see page 53) on your left, and follow the Planty path as it darts south. In front of Collegium Maius (see page 54), by ul. Gołębia (Pigeon Street), you'll find a small wooded enclave with a statue of Copernicus dating from 1900.

Cross the square and a Matejko portrait of Copernicus (see page 68) can be seen in the assembly hall of the adjacent **Collegium Novum** ❻ (ul. Gołębia 24), like Collegium Maius part of the Jagiellonian University. This neo-Gothic building, which was designed by Feliks Księżarski and built in 1883–7, replaced the Jerusalem College. Its facade features the university crests and the building is now used as its main administrative centre.

In 1939 the Nazis arrested 183 academics here that they had accused of plotting against the occupiers: many died in Sachsenhausen concentration camp. The university counts King Jan III Sobieski and Pope John Paul II among its alumni.

Church of the Sacred Heart

Continuing in a southerly direction, you will see the joyful Baroque statue of Our Lady of Mercy (Matka Boża Łaskawa) clutching a handful of broken golden arrows. Turn right into ul. Smoleńsk, where after 100m/yds you will find the 1884 **Church of the Sacred Heart of the Blessed Virgin Mary** ❼ (Kościół Niepokalanego Serca Marii), at no. 6.

TOWARDS WAWEL

Returning to the main route, walk along the leafy Planty lane for 250m/yds, passing Maria Jarema's incongruously modern 2007 fountain memorial to Chopin, which is supposed to resemble piano hammers striking (water) strings.

Crossing ul. Franciszkańska, look out for a path leading sharply left, which leads to a small square where an 1886 **statue of Grażyna and Litawor** (two characters from 'Grażyna', regarded as one of Adam Mickiewicz's finest poems) is surrounded by trees.

Archaeology Museum

Back on Planty lane, turn left again at ul. Poselska, and head towards the **Archaeology Museum** ❽ (Muzeum Archeologiczne w Krakowie, ul. Sen-

Collegium Novum

acka 3; Mon–Wed 9am–2pm, Thu 2–6pm, Fri and Sun 10am–2pm, with exceptions in winter; charge except Sun free), housed in a former friary of a Carmelite Order. Founded in 1606, this is the oldest Archaeology Museum in Poland, and contains fine exhibits, including Egyptian mummies, clothing from 70,000BC to the 14th century, and a rare relic of pre-Christian Slavonic culture: the 10th-century stone column of Światowid. It also has a pleasant walled garden.

Turn left from the museum and head back towards Planty, with Wawel directly ahead. You will you reach a small square containing a monument to the physician, translator and arts critic **Tadeusz Boy-Żeleński** (1874–1941).

Wawel's walls

On reaching ul. Podzamcze, turn right and follow the walls of Wawel Royal Castle all the way round, the tower of Wawel Cathedral (see page 39) visible on your left. You will pass Dragon's Cave (Smocza Jama, see page 41), after which the path forks. To follow Planty around take the left fork. At the next fork continue straight (rather than turning left) to arrive on ul. Bernardyńska.

Bernardine Monastery

Now walk some 300m/yds along ul. Bernardyńska, passing the **Często-chowa Seminary** ❾, built in 1928,

and head for the **Bernardine Monastery and Church** (Klasztor i Kościoł Bernardynów; also known as the Reformed Franciscan Church; open only for Mass), next to the seminary at no. 2. The Bernardine Order was established here in the 15th century by the anti-Semitic Giovanni da Capistrano. A wooden church originally stood on the site; the present, Baroque church dates from the 17th century. The church's *Madonna and Child with St Anne* is the only part of the wooden church that has survived. Later details include Mehoffer's stained-glass windows depicting the life of St Simon, a 15th-century Bernardine monk.

EASTERN PLANTY

Leave the church, turn right and, after crossing busy ul. Stradomska, turn left before darting right at the first opportunity into the eastern stretch of the Planty.

Natural History Museum

After 150m/yds, past the Royal Hotel, turn right into ul. św Sebastiana for a short detour to **Natural History Museum** ❿ (Muzeum Przyrodnicze; Mon–Fri 9am–3pm, Sat–Sun 11am–7pm; charge) at no. 9. Established in a Secessionist former public bathhouse in 1865, the museum was recently given a makeover. Top billing still goes to the world's only stuffed prehistoric woolly rhinoceros. Other exhibits include exotic animals, the evolution of

Wawel Cathedral and Castle *Bas-relief of the Częstochowa Seminary*

crabs, the rainforest and many activities to engage children.

Returning to the Planty path you can see that the churches of St Andrew the Apostle (see page 60) and Sts Peter and Paul (see page 59) are almost as impressive from the rear as from the front, as you walk north along the tree-lined lanes towards St Joseph's. Crossing ul. Dominikańska, with the Dominican Church (see page 56) on your left, you will soon pass a statue of **Narcyz Wiatr-Zawojny**, a Polish colonel shot by the Soviets in 1945.

Church of the Domincan Nuns

Crossing ul. Sienna and entering the **Grodku Garden** (Planty Na Gródku), turn left and follow the curve of ul. św Krzyża. As ul. św Krzyża crosses ul. Mikołajska you will see the entrance of the **Church and Convent of the Dominican Nuns** ⑪ (Kościół Matki Boskiej Śnieżnej i Klasztor Dominikanek; open only for Mass) at no. 21.

Founded by Duchess Anna Lubomirska in the 1630s, it possesses elegant Baroque interiors, with an ornamental vaulted ceiling, a neo-Baroque main altar and a celebrated 17th-century painting, *Matka Boska Śnieżną* (Our Lady of the Snow), a gift from Pope Urban VIII, said to have miraculous powers of healing.

Just east across ul. Na Gródku is the Gródek Hotel, whose restaurant **Restauracja Gródek** (see page 103), is a good choice for dinner. To the north on

ul. św Marka is the **Zakopianka** café and restaurant, with alfresco tables, see ②.

From the convent return to ul. Mikołajska and head north along the Planty path to return to the Florian Straszewski Obelisk. Shoppers might want to end the walk with a trip to the Galeria Krakowska (ul. Lubicz; www.galeria krakowska.pl; open late daily), the city's largest shopping mall, which is full of international brands and can be reached via the subway leading to the railway station (between the station and the main post office).

Food and Drink

① U ZALIPIANEK CAFÉ

Ul. Szewska 24; tel: 012 422 29 50; www.uzalipianek.pl; daily 9am–10pm; €€

Historic café serving a fine selection of snacks, cakes, bite-sized sandwiches and teas besides some very strong coffee. Perfect for a break while exploring Planty Gardens.

② ZAKOPIANKA

Ul. sw Marka 34; tel: 012 421 40 45; daily 11am–11pm; €€

Not the cheapest café in the city, but a thoroughly enjoyable place to spend time while circumnavigating Planty. It can get quite lively in the early evening as a drinks venue near the station.

Chairs memorial, pl. Bohaterów Getta

PODGÓRZE:
THE JEWISH GHETTO

Visit the site of Krakow's former Jewish ghetto, which for two years during World War II was a place of horrific suffering and brutality. Overlooked for decades, its historical importance is only now being fully recognised.

DISTANCE: 3.5km (2.25 miles)
TIME: A half day
START: Plac Bohaterów Getta
END: Schindler's Factory
POINTS TO NOTE: Tram 13 runs from Poczta Główna on the edge of the Old Town through Kazimierz and over the Wisła (Vistula) River into Podgórze. To follow the route taken by the Jews when the Nazis created the ghetto in 1941, walk over the Most Powstańców Śląskich.

On 3 March 1941 the Nazis set up a Jewish ghetto in Krakow's Podgórze district and herded into it the 20,000 Jews from Kazimierz who had not been deported to concentration camps. Forced to leave at less than a day's notice, they were allowed one cartload of possessions per family, and were crowded into 320 buildings between Plac Bohaterów Getta and Rynek Podgórski. From here, they were sent to Auschwitz or Płaszów. Of the almost 70,000 pre-war Jewish population of Krakow, only about 2,000 survived.

HEROES OF THE GHETTO SQUARE

If you cross Powstańców Śląskich Bridge on foot you will arrive at **Plac Bohaterów Getta ❶** (Heroes of the Ghetto Square). Once the centre of the ghetto, it features a poignant memorial to those killed, in the form of 70 randomly scattered chairs in bronze. The memorial, designed by Piotr Lewicki and Kazimierz Łatak, refers to the scene after the ghetto's liquidation in 1943, when all that remained was furniture.

Museum of National Remembrance

Ahead in the far southwest corner of the square, is **Tadeusz Pankiewicz's Eagle Pharmacy ❷**, now a museum (Apteka Pod Orłem; Plac Bohaterów Getta 18; Mon 10am–2pm, Tue–Sun 9am–5pm, closed second Tue of month; charge, free Mon). Pankiewicz was the only gentile resident of the ghetto. He operated his pharmacy throughout World War II, helping the Jews any way he could. He gave sedatives to Jewish children to keep them

The Eagle Pharmacy

A reminder of Podgórze's history

quiet during Gestapo raids, and let the ghetto's undergound movement use the pharmacy as a meeting and hiding place.

Ghetto wall

Turn right as you exit, cross ul. Na Zjeździe and head through the park to ul. Lwowska 25, where on the left is one of just two remaining sections of the **ghetto wall** ❸, which once enclosed the entire area. The small plaque reads: 'Here they lived, suffered and perished at the hands of Hitler's executioners. From here they began their final journey to the death camps.'

One survivor of the ghetto was film director Roman Polanski, who, as an 11-year old boy, escaped through a hole in the ghetto wall during its liquidation. He survived the rest of the war by hiding in the forests that surround Krakow, with the help of Polish families. In 2002 he won an Oscar for Best Director for *The Pianist*, set in the Warsaw ghetto.

UL. LIMANOWSKIEGO

Head south along ul. Lwowska until you reach ul. Limanowskiego, Podgórze's main street. Just south of here, at the top of a hill, is the 11th-century **St Benedict's Church** (Kościół św Benedykta; closed to visitors).

Turn right and follow ul. Limanowskiego as it curves around for about 300m/yds. At the corner with ul. Kra-

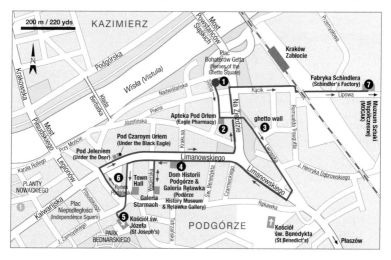

Płaszów camp memorial

kusa, you will see the **Galeria Rękawka** ❹, an outstanding contemporary art gallery, which also houses the small **Podgórze History Museum** (Dom Historii Podgórze; www.domhistoriipodgorza.pl; Tue–Fri 10am–6pm, Sat 10am–2pm; charge).

From here you can take a left into ul. Węgierska, where on the left at no. 5, inside a former synagogue, is another excellent art gallery, the **Galeria Starmach** (www.starmach.com.pl; Mon–Fri 11am–6pm).

Continue along ul. Limanowskiego. You will see the monumental neo-Gothic **St Joseph's Church** ❺ (Kościół

św Józefa; daily 7am–6pm, closed during Mass) to the left, at the far end of **Rynek Podgórski** ❻, Podgórze's former market square. On the eastern side of the square is the 19th-century former Podgórze **town hall**, next to which once stood another factory, which used Jewish slave labour.

On the square's northern side are two former inns, built in the mid-18th century: **Under the Deer** (Pod Jeleniem) is at no. 12, **Under the Black Eagle** (Pod Czarnym Orłem) is at no. 13.

For good food, however, walk a little further west, along ul. Kalwarijska, past **Plac Niepodległości** (Independence Square) to **Ogniem I Mieczem** on Planty Nowackiego, see ❶. For drinks, head back towards the river: you'll find **After Work** at the Qubus Hotel on ul. Nadwiślańska (see page 106).

SCHINDLER'S FACTORY

Retrace your steps to Plac Bohaterów Getta, cross the square and head west on ul. Kącik. Continue under the railway bridge along ul. Lipowa, to no. 4, **Schindler's Factory** ❼ (Fabryka Schindlera; www.mhk.pl to reserve advance tickets online; Apr–Oct Mon 10am–4pm, Tue–Sun 10am–8pm, Nov–Mar Mon 10am–2pm, Tue–Sun 10am–6pm, closed first Mon of every month; charge, Mon free; last admission 90 mins before closing; under-14s must be accompanied by their parents). This is where Oskar Schindler

Concentration camp

Set up in 1942 as a slave labour camp, Płaszów concentration camp was the fiefdom of Amon Göth, the brutal camp commandant portrayed by Ralph Fiennes in *Schindler's List*. Though it was not an extermination camp as such, death from disease and execution were daily occurrences, and more than 10,000 people are thought to have died here.

You can wander around the few overgrown remains of Płaszów by taking tram 13 three stops south from Plac Bohaterów Getta. Climb up the hill on foot and take a right into ul. Jerozolimska. There is a large memorial to the dead in a clearing, while Göth's crumbling former home can be seen further on at ul. Heltmana 22.

Schindler's Factory exhibit   _One of the few remaining sections of the ghetto wall_

first exploited and then protected and rescued more than 1,000 Jews of the Podgórze ghetto.

The former administrative block is now a branch of the Historical Museum of the City of Krakow, with an exhibition of Krakow under Nazi Occupation 1939–1945. Schindler's actual office forms part of this 'Factory of Memory', which makes imaginative use of eyewitness accounts, documentary film and photographs, multimedia presentations and a Survivors' Ark, created from thousands of enamel pots. The 1993 film _Schindler's List_, directed by Steven Spielberg, is a largely faithful account of life in and around the Podgórze ghetto in 1942–3.

Next door, the former factory was transformed in 2011 into the Museum of Contemporary Art in Krakow (MOCAK, Muzeum Sztuki Współczesnej w Krakowie; www.mocak.com.pl; Tue–Sun 11am–7pm; charge), which stages temporary international art exhibitions.

Food and Drink

① OGNIEM I MIECZEM

Pl. Emilia Serkowskiego 7; tel: 012 656 23 28; www.ogniemimieczem.pl; Mon–Sat noon–11.30pm, Sun noon–10pm; €€€

Boar and duck top the bill at this 17th-century huntsman's paradise decked out with trophies and animal skins.

Oskar Schindler

Schindler (1908–74) was born to a wealthy family in the Sudetenland (present-day Czech Republic) and was childhood friends with the Jewish family next door. He moved to Krakow at the outbreak of the war (allegedly to avoid conscription), and bought a factory, which he staffed with cheap Jewish labour. Producing bomb casings for the Nazis, he grew rich, yet he frittered away much of his money on women and black-market goods, which he used to buy the local SS officers' loyalty.

After witnessing the liquidation of the Podgórze ghetto in 1943, Schindler vowed to do what he could for 'his' Jews, and managed to have his factory declared a sub-camp of Płaszów concentration camp. As the Red Army closed in on Krakow, however, his factory was forced to close and his Jews were slated for deportation to an extermination camp. Schindler persuaded the authorities to let him take 1,200 workers to a new factory at Brunnlitz, close to his home town, drawing up his list of workers who would join him.

Brunnlitz was freed by the Red Army in May 1945, though Schindler had fled the night before – a Nazi party member since 1939, he would likely have been shot. He lived in Argentina until 1958, when he returned to Germany. When he died in 1974, he was bankrupt, living off the charity of those he had saved.

Concrete colonnade on Plac Centralny

NOWA HUTA

Take a tram to Nowa Huta, a 1950s' experiment in social engineering. This town and steelworks built to an entirely Socialist Realist concept 10km (6 miles) east of the city centre was devised to redress what the Soviet Union saw as Krakow's 'class imbalance'.

DISTANCE: 3km (2 miles)
TIME: A half day
START: Plac Centralny
END: Arka Pana Church
POINTS TO NOTE: To get to Nowa Huta you should take tram no. 4 from Krakow's main railway station. The journey takes no more than 35 minutes. A taxi takes considerably less and costs around 35zł each way.

Conceived by Poland's Communist authorities in collusion with the Soviet Union at the end of the 1940s, Nowa Huta (New Steelworks) was constructed to create both a modern steelworks to support the industrialisation of southern Poland, and a proletarian base in Krakow: until then Krakow was seen (somewhat mistakenly) as a city without a working class.

Built mainly from 1949 to 1956, the architecture of Nowa Huta is a mix of neo-Renaissance, neoclassical and Utilitarian. Ignored by visitors for years, the town has attracted something of a cult following recently both for Communist nostalgics and for students of architecture. For the casual visitor it provides a telling insight into how the 'utopia' many Communists aspired to create might have looked.

CENTRAL SQUARE

If coming from Krakow by tram, get off at **Plac Centralny ❶**, the centre of Nowa Huta. All streets fan out from here, and the scene – of five almost identical, wide, tree-lined avenues and smart blocks – is immediately impressive.

Designed by a collective of Polish architects, the square was the first part of Nowa Huta to be completed, in 1956. Looking around you will note that the southern side of the square lacks any buildings: a giant cultural centre was planned for the site but was never built.

Before heading further into Nowa Huta, cross over to the southern side of the square and take a quick detour east for 100m/yds along al. Jana Pawła II for a glimpse at the blocks of the **Na Skarpie ❷** district. Built in the

Our Lord's Ark Church bells   *A street named after Pope John Paul II*

1970s, they are considered by most to be an eyesore.

MAIN STREET

Walking back to Plac Centralny, head directly north along **al. Róż**, Nowa Huta's main thoroughfare. After 50m/yds it widens to form a large square, often used today for concerts. The neoclassical apartment blocks that line the square are the finest in the town and were reserved for the highest echelons of steelwork management.

The taller building on your left, on the corner of al. Przyjazni, and sporting a rather sublime loggia, is Nowa Huta's **former town hall** ❸. The grand town hall designed for this square was never built and the statue of Lenin that stood here was finally removed in 1989, having survived the residents' spirited attempt to blow it up in 1979.

This is also the location of Stylowa, the oldest restaurant and one of the very few places in Nowa Huta to eat that isn't a milk bar, see ❶.

Cross al. Przyjazni and detour right into one of the many little **parks** that dot the town. Nowa Huta was designed so that a third of its area would be green space. Stroll through to the other side of the park, (there are benches if you need a rest) and across to the **History of the Nowa Huta Quarter museum** ❹ (Dzieje Nowy Huty, os. Słoneczne 16; www.mhk.pl; Apr–Oct Tue–Sun 9.30am–5pm, Nov–Mar Tue, Thu, Fri 9am–4pm, Wed, Sat–Sun 10am–5pm; charge, Wed free), staging exhibitions on the town's history and culture.

LUDOWY THEATRE

Head north a further 100m/yds along al. Róż to the junction with al. Żeromskiego. Turn left and head northwest, taking the right-hand fork after 50m/yds. On your left, set back from the street, is the **Ludowy Theatre** ❺ (Teatr Ludowy; os. Teatralne 34), a low-rise

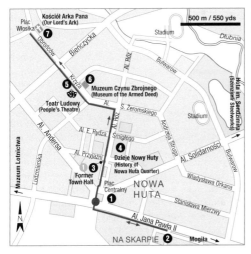

Inside Our Lord's Ark Church

building that is one of many in Nowa Huta sadly showing signs of neglect. Completed in 1955, the theatre has long been associated with avant-garde productions.

City of rebels

Nowa Huta was designed to be a city of 100,000 of the proletariat (today's population is approximately 250,000), with its inhabitants all loyal supporters of the Communist party. Like much about Nowa Huta, however, not everything went according to plan. The workers of the steel plant have often been a major thorn in the side of Poland's authorities, both before and after the fall of Communism, most notably during Martial Law in 1981.

As Nowa Huta expanded in the 1970s, and huge tobacco and cement factories also opened nearby, new housing had to be built quickly. As a result, building standards dropped, and the size of apartments shrank. With the general drop in living standards throughout Poland in the late 1970s, Nowa Huta's workers came out on strike in support of the Solidarity movement in 1981. The authorities had to use force to quell the riots – killing a steelworks apprentice during a demonstration in 1983.

Ironically, the fall of Communism and the onset of capitalism may see the death of Nowa Huta. The steelworks face a precarious future.

MUSEUM OF THE ARMED DEED

Cross the street and the tank that faces you marks the entrance to the **Museum of the Armed Deed ❻** (Muzeum Czynu Zbrojnego; os. Górali 23; www.mczz.3-2-1.pl; Mon–Fri 10am–3pm), a rather touching exhibition devoted to those from the Nowa Huta area who have fought and died for Poland.

ARKA PANA

Exit the museum and turn right, walking a further 300m/yds to Plac Włosika, where you will find the startling **Arka Pana** or **Our Lord's Ark ❼** (Kościół Arka Pana; ul. Obrońców Krzyża 1; www.arka pana.pl; daily 6am–6pm, closed during Mass), the first church to be built in Nowa Huta, between 1967 and 1977.

Designing a socialist utopia meant no room for churches, and for decades the authorities refused repeated calls from locals to build one. Finally, Nowa Huta's faithful took things into their own hands and began construction of the church.

Designed by Cracovian Wojciech Pietrzyk to resemble Noah's Ark resting on Mount Ararat, Arka Pana was built brick by brick, work often stopping for months due to a lack of materials. It was consecrated in 1977 by the then Cardinal Wojtyła, soon to become Pope John Paul II, who had dug the first foundations as Archbishop of Krakow 10 years

Aviation Museum plane   *Nowa Huta is named after the steelworks*

earlier, and helped prevent its demolition by angry authorities.

Among the highlights inside are a huge figure of Christ flying up to Heaven by Bronisław Chromy, the tabernacle containing a fragment of rutile crystal brought back from the moon by the crew of Apollo 11 and a statue of Mary made from 10kg (22lbs) of shrapnel removed from Polish soldiers wounded at Monte Cassino.

THE STEELWORKS

To get back to Krakow's Old Town, turn left from the church, then right onto ul. Bieńczycka and up to its junction with Al. Andersa, where you can take bus 502 or tram no. 1 at the roundabout. However, for many people a visit to Nowa Huta is not complete without a trip to the town's raison d'être, the steelworks, although note that they are off limits to the public.

To get there, head back to Plac Centralny, and take tram no. 4 to the Kombinat stop, directly in front of the steelworks' entrance. You can't miss it: enormous letters framed by monumental twin buildings (the administration centre) tell you that this is **Huta im. Sendzimira** (Szenzimir Steelworks).

Nowadays owned by the Arcelor-Mittal group, during Communism the steelworks carried the name of Lenin, and its workers were famously militant. At its peak in the 1970s the Nowa Huta steelworks were producing 6.5 million tonnes of steel annually. Today, output is much reduced and it employs a little more than 10 percent of the staff it once did.

If you want to eat in Nowa Huta, your best option is the **Santorini** restaurant at the hotel of the same name (see page 111). From the steelworks, take bus no. 174 two stops to Bulwarowa.

Just west of Nowa Huta is the Polish Aviation Museum (Muzeum Lotnictwa Polskiego; al. Jana Pawła II 39; www.muzeumlotnictwa.pl; Wed–Sun 9am–5pm, Tue outdoor exhibition only 9am–5pm; charge, Tue free). Alongside the rusty Sovietera MIG fighters are some real highlights, including a Sopwith Camel and one of the world's few remaining Spitfires in perfect condition.

To get there take tram no. 10 to the awf stop. If you're coming from the city centre then walk back the way you came a short distance – the museum is set back from the road through a small wooded park. If in doubt, ask a local to point the way.

Food and Drink

① STYLOWA

Os. Centrum 3; tel: 012 644 26 19; http://stylowa-nowahuta.pl; daily 9am–11pm; €€€
This historic restaurant, with an interior like a time warp, serves simple, tasty Polish dishes, such as herring in sour cream, cooked in the traditional way.

Gubałówka wooden houses

ZAKOPANE

This is a pretty holiday resort in the Carpathian Mountains; its 30,000 inhabitants are Górale, or highlanders, and for more than a century this has been a traditional retreat for intellectuals and Poland's winter sports capital.

DISTANCE: 100km (62 miles) one way from Krakow; town centre tour: 3.5km (2 miles)

TIME: A full day

START: Grand Hotel Stamary

END: Gubałówka

POINTS TO NOTE: Most of Zakopane's sights can just about be visited on a day trip from Krakow, although if you want to hike or ski then you should stay at least one night. Zakopane can be reached from Krakow by train or bus. The bus is recommended, as the train is painfully slow. There are a number of private bus companies of varying comfort operating the route; they depart from Krakow's main bus station and deposit passengers at the Grand Hotel Stamary. The journey by bus takes just over two hours in good weather.

The little town of **Zakopane** is known for its beautiful mountain scenery in summer and prime skiing in winter. Set at the foot of the Tatra Mountains, Zakopane was, from the 16th century, a village of sheep farmers. The Górale people who live here speak their own dialect and maintain traditional customs, including folk music and dancing. The local architecture is characterised by wooden buildings adorned with carvings and painted rustic motifs.

A symbol of resistance

Poland 'discovered' Zakopane in the 1870s, when a Warsaw doctor, Tytus Chałubiński, visited what was then a village. The first hotel was built in 1885 to accommodate artists and intellectuals inspired by the highlanders' indomitable independence – they were seen as a symbol of resistance to the occupations of Poland by Prussia, Russia and Austria. Zakopane became a bohemian centre at the start of the 20th century, with a guest list starring, among others, the Nobel Prize-winning novelist Henryk Sienkiewicz and the concert pianist Ignacy Paderewski. Some of Poland's leading artists established permanent homes here, and elements of highland culture began to appear in the work of composers such as Karol Szymanowski and writers such as Jan Kasprowicz. The painter,

Enjoying a drink and a mountain view

architect and critic Stanisław Witkiewicz was a key figure in propagating the 'Zakopane style' of wooden buildings.

TOWN CENTRE

Having arrived at the bus station in front of the **Grand Hotel Stamary ❶**, you might want to relax for a while in the hotel's **Café Stamary**, see ①. From here, turn right and head along ul. Kościuszki as it passes through the town centre's largest park, the **Rówień Krupówka ❷**.

Tatra Museum

Cross al. 3 Maja and continue to ul. Krupówki, the town's busy main thoroughfare. Turn right and walk along to the **Tatra Museum ❸** (Muzeum Tatrzańskie; ul. Krupówki 10; www.muzeumtatrzanskie.pl; Oct–Apr Wed–Sat 9am–5pm; May–Sept Wed–Sat 10am–6pm), Sun 9am–3pm, also May–Sept Tue; charge). Itself an example of an early Zakopane-style building, it has fine collections of folk art and natural history, and more besides: two reconstructions of ancient mountaintop dwellings delight kids of all ages

Two parish churches

Opposite is the 1877–96 neo-Romanesque **Krupówki Parish Church ❹** (Krupówki Kościół Parafialny). Witkiewicz

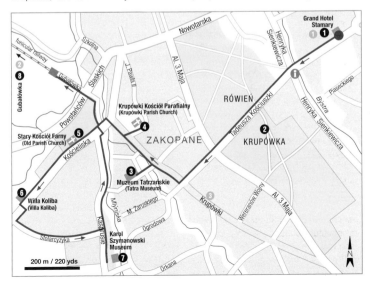

Local husky

designed its **Chapels of John the Baptist and Our Lady Mary of the Rosary** (Kaplica Jana Chrzciciela and Matki Bożej Różańcowej), as well as the stained-glass windows and polychromy, in the Zakopane style.

Turn right into ul. Krupówki and then left into ul. Kościeliska. On your right is the town's oldest church, the mid-19th-century **Old Parish Church** ❺ (Stary Kościół Farny also known as Kościół Pęksowy Brzyek). In the cemetery here you'll find the tombstones of famous figures, including Witkiewicz and Chałubiński, as well as that of Helena Marusarzówna, a

Polish ski champion shot by the Nazis in 1941 for being a member of the Polish resistance.

Villa Koliba

About 100m/yds further along is the **Villa Koliba** ❻ (Willa Koliba; ul. Kościeliska 18; www.muzeumtatrzanskie.pl; Wed–Sat 9am–5pm (Jul–Aug 10am–6pm), Sun 9am–3pm; charge), built in 1893 by Witkiewicz in a design inspired by a highlander's cottage. It is one of the few surviving original 19th-century Zakopane hunting lodges.

Karol Szymanowski Museum

From here, cross the road and walk along ul. Stolarczyka to ul. Kasprusie. To your right, on the other side of the road, is the Villa Atma's **Karol Szymanowski Museum** ❼ (ul. Kasprusie 19; www.muzeum.krakow.pl; Tue–Sun 10am–5pm, also May–Oct Fri until 7pm; charge). The villa was home in the

---

Hiking and skiing

This region is popular with hikers – numerous well-marked trails lead to the gorgeous Alpine scenery of the Tatra Mountains. All routes are well marked, but you should not set off without a good map, available at tourist information centres and good Krakow bookshops.

Most of Zakopane's 3 million annual visitors, however, come to ski, with good snow conditions from December to mid-April. Note that the ski runs are split into four separate areas, none of which interlinks. When the snow is deep (more than 6m/18ft) the best skiing is on Kasprowy Wierch to the south of the resort, accessed by Poland's first cable car, installed in 1936 but now replaced with an up-to-date, high-tech version (www.pkl.pl).

Tatra Museum   *The Old Parish Church*

1930s to the composer Szymanowski (1882–1937).

UP TO GUBAŁÓWKA

Walking back to the town centre along ul. Kaprusie, cross the small park, then pass through the town's large **market** and head up on to Na Gubałówkę. At no. 2 is a wonderful shop and **gallery** selling paintings of Zakopane and its mountains (do not expect bargains) as well as local painted glass (the town has a history of glass-painting).

Funicular and food
A short distance up the hill is a **funicular** (www.pkl.pl; daily, 9am–8pm, and to 9.45pm in school holidays in Dec, Jan, Feb, May, Jul and Aug, Oct 9am–7pm, Nov and early Dec 9am–6pm; charge), which whisks skiers, bobsledders and hikers up to **Gubałówka** ❽, once a tiny mountain village, now a mini resort-with-in-a-resort. In winter there are some short and easy ski runs from here, while in summer there is a 750m/yd-long dry bobsleigh run, an adventure rope park and long hikes across the Tatras.

The **Gubałzerria restaurant** at the top of the funicular is a scenic spot to eat, see ❷, or a place to rest tired legs if you have walked up the mountain. The route is steep – it can be done by the very fit in around an hour, weather-permitting, but is not recommended for young children or the elderly, or for anyone in bad weather.

Alternatively, head back into town to ul. Krupówki for hearty Górale cooking at **Karczma Sabala**, see ❸.

Food and Drink

❶ CAFÉ STAMARY
Ul. Kościuszki 19; tel: 018 202 45 12; www.stamary.pl; daily 9am-midnight; €€€
After a journey from Krakow, you may wish to refuel with coffee and cake in this café, conveniently located in the imposing Grand Hotel Stamary beside the bus station.

❷ GUBAŁZZERIA
Ul. Gubałówka 2; tel: 018 206 13 14; daily 9am–10pm peak times, closes at 7pm off peak; €€
At the top of the Gubałówka, this mountain retreat with waitresses dressed like Heidi offers cheap and cheerful Polish dishes and pizza in a wood and glass building. The views over the mountains are terrific. On the down side, you have to pay for the toilets.

❸ KARCZMA SABALA
Ul. Krupówki 11; tel: 018 201 50 92; www.sabala.zakopane.pl; daily 11am–midnight; €€
Places like this are what Poland's mountains are all about. A wooden villa (with hotel rooms on the upper floors), good food, a great atmosphere and decent prices. The food is local: Górale specialities include *patelnia bacowska*, a lamb stew. The staff are friendly and speak English.

Reconstructed barracks at Auschwitz II–Birkenau

AUSCHWITZ

The infamous Nazi death camp is now a Unesco World Heritage Site and museum. From 1940–45 between 1.1 and 1.5 million people – almost a quarter of all those killed in the Holocaust – were murdered here.

> **DISTANCE:** 60km (37 miles) west of Krakow
> **TIME:** A full day
> **POINTS TO NOTE:** Oświęcim is served by regular buses from Krakow's bus station (see www.visitauschwitz.eu for timetables). The journey takes about 1 hour 30 mins. Buses to Krakow depart opposite the memorial reception area. Less frequent trains from Krakow Dworzec Główny stop at Oświęcim but the station is about a 25-min walk from the camp. Snacks and drinks are on sale around the main entrance, but meals are not available. Bring water in summer.

The town of **Oświęcim** (Auschwitz) will always be synonymous with the Holocaust. It is now an industrial centre south of Katowice, Poland's key industrial conurbation. The site of a castle in the 12th century, it became the capital of an independent dukedom in 1317 and part of Poland in 1457. In the years of Poland's partition (1772–1918) the town was part of Austria.

Creation of Auschwitz-Birkenau

Shortly after invading Poland in 1939, the Nazis built the Auschwitz-Birkenau concentration camp. The largest such complex in the country, it comprised two camps covering 172 hectares (425 acres). Auschwitz was a slave-labour camp largely reserved for political prisoners, members of the resistance and other 'opponents' of the Nazi regime – mainly Poles and Germans; Auschwitz II-Birkenau, opened in 1942, was used as an extermination camp.

The killings

Transported in cattle trucks from all over Europe, between 1.1 and 1.5 million prisoners from more than 25 nations lost their lives here. Though the vast majority of victims were Jews, there were numerous Polish, Russian and Roma gypsy inmates, too. Many died as a result of slave labour, hunger, illness and torture. The genocide peaked in 1942, when the gas chambers were killing several thousand people every day.

Glasses that once belonged to inmates

Liberated by the Red Army

Before retreating in 1944, the Nazis began destroying the evidence of their horrific crimes. They detonated the crematoria and some camp buildings, but did not have enough time to destroy the gas chambers. The camp was liberated by Russia's Red Army in 1945.

AUSCHWITZ I

Auschwitz-Birkenau (www.auschwitz. org.pl; Apr, Oct 8am–5pm, May, Sept 8am–6pm, June–Aug 8am–7pm, Mar, Nov 8am–4pm, Dec–Feb 8am–3pm; children under 12 should not watch the introductory film, though they are admitted; entrance to the camps is free, but there is a charge for the introductory film and for guided tours) was made a national museum in 1947 and a World Heritage Site in 1979.

A visit to Auschwitz begins with a visit to the **reception and information centre**. Here you can enquire about **tours**, as well as watch the chilling **introduc-**

tory film. At busy times in the summer, visitors may be required to join a tour. It is a good idea to buy a copy of the official guidebook, which shows the suggested route around both camps. Auschwitz and Auschwitz II (Birkenau) are 3km (2 miles) apart: a free shuttle bus connects the two, departing at 30-minute intervals.

'Arbeit Macht Frei'

From the reception, make your way past the former SS Guard House and through the notorious **camp entrance gate**, complete with the infamous camp motto, *Arbeit Macht Frei* (Work Makes You Free). Passing the former kitchens on your right, in front of you is **Block 4**, which contains the first main exhibition, outlining the story of the camp, as well as the creation of Zyklon B, the gas used to kill so many prisoners. In a room at the rear are the remains of more than 7 tonnes of human hair, shorn from prisoners as they entered the camp and originally intended for German clothing factories but abandoned along with the camp in January 1945.

Next door is **Block 5**, which displays belongings stripped from prisoners as they arrived. Most poignant are the children's shoes and toys, while the piles of glasses and artificial limbs are equally harrowing. Daily life in Auschwitz is covered in **Blocks 6 and 7**, and includes exhibitions of camp prisoner art.

The infamous motto that greeted prisoners upon arrival

Wall of Death

At the far end of the camp (between Blocks 10 and 11 – the last blocks on your left) is the **Wall of Death**, where daily prisoners were shot for breaking the smallest of camp regulations. **Block 10** (closed to visitors) was itself an awful place: medical experiments were carried out here, mainly on female prisoners, many of whom died as a result.

Block 11 was the camp's prison, in which many of the pitch black cells were so small that prisoners could neither sit or stand. Few survived in here for more than a few days. Though many of the cells were destroyed, you can visit that of Father Kolbe, a Polish priest who died here after changing places with a Jewish prisoner who survived because of him. It was in the cellars of Block 11 that the Nazis carried out their first experiments with Zyklon B, in 1941.

National Memorials

From Block 11 visitors turn right and head back towards the main entrance, passing

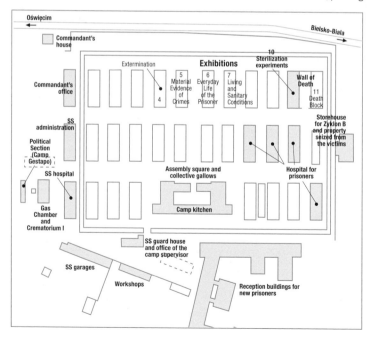

The Gates of Hell

various blocks given over to **National Memorials**. These are designed and maintained by memorial groups from many of the countries whose citizens died here, and change frequently. Ask about the latest exhibitions at the reception centre on arrival.

GAS CHAMBER

After walking through **Roll Call Square**, where – until the camp's population became unmanageable – roll call would be held three times a day, continue to the end of the row of blocks to a reconstruction of the **gas chamber and crematoria**. The gas chamber functioned from 1941–3, and was used to put to death those prisoners who were no longer fit for work. After the creation of the extermination camp at **Auschwitz II-Birkenau** in 1942, the gas chamber at Auschwitz was dismantled and the building used as an air-raid shelter by the SS.

The **gallows** in front of the gas chamber was used to hang camp commandant Rudolf Höss in 1947. From here, follow the path 200m/yds back to the reception centre, to catch the bus to Auschwitz II-Birkenau.

AUSCHWITZ II-BIRKENAU

If you take the bus to Birkenau you will be deposited at the **Gates of Hell**, one of the few parts of the camp left intact. Featured in a number of films that have been set in the camp – including *Schindler's List* –

they are now almost as infamous as the *Arbeit Macht Frei* gates in Auschwitz I. Follow the original railway tracks through gates to the site of the unloading ramp, where the trains carrying Jews from all over Europe would arrive, and where selection would take place: those fit for work would be sent for processing; those declared unfit would immediately be sent to the camp's gas chambers.

In terms of camp remains, there is very little to see at Birkenau, and there is no suggested route. It is a place of reflection and remembrance. Most visitors, however, choose to walk the length of the unloading ramp to the remains of the gas chamber and crematoria, where there is a simple memorial to the victims of the camp. To the left of the ramp are two reconstructed women's barracks, which show the appalling conditions inmates had to endure. Hundreds, and at times more than a thousand, people shared one barrack house.

From the gas chamber, walk 300m/yds northwest to the 'sauna' (another reconstruction) where those chosen for work were disinfected before being assigned to barracks rife with disease.

From here, walk past the Ash Pond – one of many pits outside the camp where the ashes of prisoners were dumped – and trace the outline of the camp back to the Gates of Hell: its scale is terrifying. Even more so is the knowledge that it was to be extended. The vast area behind the Ash Pond was known as Mexico, intended for expansion but never completed.

There are many kilometres of tunnels in the mine

WIELICZKA SALT MINE

Explore a centuries-old subterranean world as you venture down into Poland's oldest working salt mine. Listed as a Unesco World Heritage Site in 1978, the mine now incorporates museums, galleries, chapels, burial grounds and even an underground restaurant.

DISTANCE: (Mine tour) 3.5km (2.5 miles)

TIME: A half day

POINTS TO NOTE: Wieliczka is 10km (6 miles) from Krakow. There are trains from Krakow, but the journey is quicker by bus 304 which leaves from ul. Kurniki opposite Galeria Krakowska, or by minibus departing opposite Krakow's Main Post Office at the junction of ul. Westerplatte and ul. Starowiślna. Get off at the junction of ul. Dembowskiego and ul. Daniłowicza in Wieliczka. Regarding tours of the mine, if you have a fear of confined spaces, this is probably not an expedition for you. It's possible to leave the tour at only a few locations, and even if you do get out early, you may need to wait your turn for the cramped cage lift to get you back up to ground level. Remember the mine is at a constant 15°C (59°F), so dress accordingly; layers are sensible. Wear sturdy shoes, too, as there are lots of steps to climb.

The town of Wieliczka, which received its charter in 1289, developed around the lucrative salt-mining trade. The salt was initially obtained from springs that bubbled up in the area, a process that was so successful that, by the 14th and 15th centuries, this had become one of the continent's most important mining towns.

Visiting the mine

Wieliczka Salt Mine (Kopalnia Soli Wieliczka; ul. Daniłowicza 10; www.wieliczka-saltmine.com; daily Apr–Oct 7.30am–7.30pm, Nov–Mar 8am–5pm;

Altar in St Kinga's Chapel   *Sculpture of Casimir the Great*

by guided tour only, available in different languages; charge) has a 3.5km (2 mile) tourist trail that descends to level three, some 135m (443ft) underground. It makes for a moderately strenuous two-hour tour. The descent into the mine is by stairway, although lift access can be arranged. The more physically demanding Miner's Route lasts for three hours.

Sanatorium

Since the mid-19th century, when salt baths were first recognised for their healing potential, Wieliczka has also been a **sanatorium**. Today its underground chambers are still used for the treatment of respiratory illnesses, particularly asthma, and allergies. Working, too, as a modern-day health resort, visitors can book both overnight stays and day treatments. Tours of the treatment centre are available.

LEVEL ONE

After being sorted into language groups in the reception area (this can involve a wait of up to an hour if you have not pre-booked), you walk down the 378 steps of the **Daniłowicz Shaft**, sunk in 1635, to level one. The shaft itself continues to level six, at a depth of 243m (800ft). At the bottom, you will be cramped into a tiny space for five minutes while the guide presents some basic information about the mine. From here you are led to the **Copernicus Chamber**, a huge room dedicated to the astronomer Copernicus, who visited the mine in the 15th century while a student at the Jagiellonian University. Next you pass through the Baroque **St Anthony's Chapel**, which hosted its first service in 1698: it is the oldest of the mine's chapels. Almost all of the chapel's decorations and sculptures are made of salt.

There are more salt sculptures in the **Janowice Chamber** next door, while the **Burnt Chamber** is a chilling reminder of the dangers of salt mining: an explosion here in the 19th century killed a number of miners. The tight **Sielec Chamber** is next. Here you can see a number of tools used by salt miners over the centuries.

Moving to the other side of the mine, the enormous, impressive **Casimir the Great Chamber** displays an original horse-powered harness used to haul salt from lower levels, yet is merely a taster of what comes next: the **Pieskowa Skała Chamber**, one of the largest in the mine, which links level one with level two, 65m (213ft) below. Be warned: the stairs are very steep in places.

LEVEL TWO

In the **Kunegunda Traverse**, you can see the original wooden drains as well as waxworks of miners hauling salt through the tunnels.

The **Holy Cross Chapel** features a Baroque wooden crucifix dating from

St John's Chapel

the 17th century, after which you will visit the cathedral-like **St Kinga's Chapel**, probably the most impressive of the mine's places of worship. It features a number of bas-reliefs, all carved in salt by miners and depicting scenes from the New Testament, as well as a pulpit (also in salt) in the approximate shape of Wawel Hill. The chapel is renowned for its incredible acoustics.

From the chapel you are led downhill towards the **Erazm Barącz Chamber**, filled with one of the mine's salt lakes. The water here is 9m (30ft) deep. As you walk around the precarious wooden gallery you will wonder how on earth it was built.

Continuing downhill, through the **Michałowice** and **Drozdowice Chambers**, you arrive at the deep **Weimar Chamber**, excavated in the early 20th century and named after the Prince of Weimar who visited with the German writer and poet J.W. von Goethe in the 17th century. It features some impressive salt sculptures in the various recesses and a deep brine lake at the bottom; note that the staircase that hugs the walls as you descend to level three is extremely steep.

LEVEL THREE

A monument commemorating Józef Piłsudski (the World War I soldier and statesman who is credited with restoring independence to Poland in 1918), carved in rock salt by the miner sculptor Stanisław Anioł in 1997, dominates the upper part of the **Piłsudski Chamber**. One of the first parts of the mine to be opened up as a tourist trail (by the Austrians in the 1830s), it leads past the Poniatowski Traverse to the 36m (118ft) high **Staszic Chamber**, dedicated to Stanisław Staszic, a 19th-century geologist whose bust (in salt of course) is at the top of the chamber. From here, a glass lift brings you down to the floor of the chamber.

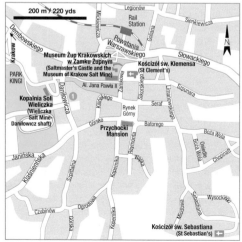

Souvenir lights from the mine

The surreal Kunegunda Gallery

Coming into the Wisla Chamber you will find access to facilities and the chance for a rest, and maybe view a temporary exhibition. The first part of the tour ends here in **Witold Budryk Chamber**, today a restaurant, **Karczma Górnicza**, see ①. At this point you are 125m (410ft) below the surface. There is an opportunity to buy souvenirs here, too. Beyond here is the wooden altar of **St John's Chapel**, where private masses and occasional weddings are held.

If you wish to leave the tour at this stage, you follow the signs and are whizzed back up to the top by lift. If you continue to the Krakow Saltworks Museum – run by a different company but included in your ticket– you'll visit a further 16 chambers full of artefacts, mining equipment and miners' clothing, as well as works of art, including paintings by the Polish artist, Jan Matejko. There is also a chamber displaying the most beautiful salt crystals.

SALTMASTER'S CASTLE

While you are exploring Wieliczka, it is also well worth discovering the neighbouring **Saltmaster's Castle** (Museum Żup Krakowskich w Zamku Żupnym; www.muzeum.wieliczka.pl; May–Sep Tue–Sun 9am–8pm, Oct–Apr 8.30am–3.30pm; charge, Sat free). As you leave the mine, the castle grounds are directly opposite. Originally a 13th-century fortress that was turned into a Renaissance castle in the 16th century, this is the country's sole example of medieval architecture relating to salt mining and trading. To see an exhibition focusing on the ancient and early medieval history of Wieliczka and its surroundings, you have to go underground once more – it's in the original 13th- to 15th-century cellars. The 16th-century Gothic hall, with a vaulted ceiling supported by a single pillar, is hung with portraits of the castle's former salt lords. A collection of salt cellars reflects various styles from the 18th to the 20th centuries. The display also features Polish and other European porcelain.

Other buildings within the castle complex include a 14th-century Gothic bastion and defensive walls, a warehouse, guardhouse and kitchen.

Food and Drink

① KARCZMA GÓRNICZA

The underground Miners' Tavern could be one of Europe's great tourist traps, but thankfully the mine's management have kept it simple and inexpensive. The briny atmosphere stimulates the appetite, so prepare to tuck into huge portions of Polish food, such as *zurek* (rye soup) with sausage or *bigos*. There is also a children's menu. Groups can pre-order food so it is ready and waiting at the end of their tour.

DIRECTORY

Hand-picked hotels and restaurants to suit all budgets and tastes, organised by area, plus select nightlife listings, an alphabetical listing of practical information, a language guide and an overview of the best books and films to give you a flavour of the city.

Grand Hotel bed

ACCOMMODATION

At one time Krakow's accommodation scene was characterised by shabby remnants of Poland's communist past and its state-run lodgings ruled with iron-fist discipline. This once-dormant hotel scene exploded into life with the boom of the budget flight, and today visitors find themselves spoilt for choice. At the top end, there is everything from mega-brand chains to boutique hotels, while lower down the pecking order Krakow has plenty of family-run guesthouses, B&Bs and self-catering apartments and some of Europe's best hostels.

Accommodation will likely be your biggest expense in Krakow. While rooms are most expensive in high season, Krakow's emergence in recent times as a year-round destination means that hotel prices stay fairly stable throughout the year. A lack of business travellers means that few hotels lower their rates at weekends either. Almost all hotels of note include breakfast in the price, with a few charging extra and the absolute minority offering no breakfast at all.

Booking in advance is advisable year-round, and essential during the high season, which kicks off around the start of June and finishes towards the end of September. If you want to stay in Zakopane, which receives 50 times its population in tourists annually, it's even more vital to book in the high seasons of summer (June–Sept) or winter (Christmas–Mar).

Around Main Market Square

Amadeus
Ul. Mikołajska 20; tel: 012 429 60 70; www.hotel-amadeus.pl; €€€€
Numerous celebrities from Prince Charles to the Russian dancer Mikhail Baryshnikov have chosen to stay here, giving an indication of the hotel's high standards. Expect sublime service, large rooms full of rich furniture, and fine common areas bursting with genuine Mozart memorabilia, in honour of the name. And it all comes at reasonable – if hardly cheap – prices.

Elektor
Ul. Szpitalna 28; tel: 012 423 23 17; www.hotelelektor.pl; €€€
A Krakow legend, where the draw of the enormous double rooms with separate lounge area has proven to be irresistible for any number of high-rolling visitors. Simply furnished, the rooms are

> Price guide for a double room for one night with breakfast:
> €€€€ = over 600zł
> €€€ = 425–600zł
> €€ = 250–425zł
> € = under 250zł

Neo-Baroque interior at the Grand Hotel

not perhaps as luxurious as they once were, but they offer excellent value for money, and the suites especially are almost always reserved months in advance.

La Fontaine

Ul. Sławkowska 1; tel: 012 422 65 64; www.bblafontaine.com; €€

Provided you've got a strong pair of legs to conquer the stairwell, La Fontaine is a highly credible self-catering option. Rooms are decorated in red shades, and while the decor can't be considered snappy, you get a highly central location in return for your money.

Grand Hotel

Ul. Sławkowska 5–7; tel: 012 424 08 00; www.grand.pl; €€€€

A stone's throw from Main Market Square, the Grand is a showcase of neo-Baroque interior design. Every room and suite is individually decorated and all have great bathrooms, WiFi and discreetly positioned televisions. If you can stretch your wallet, go for one of the six suites: the Louis XVIth-style Fireplace Suite is a favourite. The hotel has two restaurants as well as the Vienna Café and Bar. The Mirror Hall restaurant is a showcase of elegant Secessionist style, with a stained-glass dome and ornate galleries at the mezzanine level, while the Piano restaurant offers more intimate spaces. In the restaurants, classic dishes are served by waiters familiar with old-world standards of courtesy.

Staff members will help translate menus that feature Polish specialities such as sole Walewska, trout and perch dishes alongside modern European favourites.

Grodek

Ul. Na Gródku 4; tel: 012 431 90 30; www.donimirski.com; €€€€

During construction of the Grodek in 2005, an important medieval archaeological site was unearthed next door, and was immediately incorporated into the plans as a museum of archaeology. It is such attention to detail – no request is too big – that sets the Grodek apart; that and the wonderful, award-winning interior design: a modern take on Old Krakow with a cheeky Bohemian twist. A highlight of any visit to Krakow is a visit to the hotel's exquisite restaurant, which offers opulent surroundings and new flavours and twists on classic Polish cooking.

Hostel Rynek 7

Rynek Główny 7; tel: 012 431 16 98; http://hostelrynek7.pl; €

Making square-located lodging accessible to all pockets, this clean, friendly venue has windows opening onto the Cloth Hall. With the exception of a couple of doubles, rooms follow the stack-a-backpacker mentality, with wood-framed bunks squeezed into long narrow rooms.

Pałac Bonerowski

Ul. św. Jana 1; tel: 012 374 13 00; www.palacbonerowski.pl; €€€€

One of the most historic buildings in Krakow, which in the 17th century served as both home and official headquarters of King Jan Sobieski, has been carefully converted into one of the city's best hotels. There are eight simple but elegantly furnished rooms and six exquisite suites, and if their size is not immediately impressive, the decor and extras, such as the views of the Main Market Square, marble bathrooms and what they claim is 'Europe's longest chandelier', are.

Pod Róża

Ul. Floriańska 14; tel: 012 424 33 00; www.podroza.hotel.com.pl; €€€

This elegant, centrally located hotel is Krakow's oldest. It has some impressive period features such as the mid-19th-century neoclassical entrance, and every corner is filled with antiques. Recent renovation has done nothing to diminish its historic atmosphere. Of its two restaurants, the Italian, Amarone, is the most talked about. Its main, atrium-style, dining room tricks you into thinking you are sitting under a Roman sky, while two smaller dining rooms cater for those seeking a more intimate ambiance. Though the menu, changed seasonally, reads like standard Italian fare, the pasta is made in house, and the dishes, such as pappardelle with wild mushrooms, lamb osso bucco and pannacotta with strawberries, are full of genuine Italian flavour. An extensive Italian wine list is another bonus. Elegantly dressed tables attract a suitably dressed-up crowd.

Saski

Ul. Sławkowska 3; tel: 012 421 42 22; www.hotelsaski.com.pl; €€

This venerable 16th-century building comes with a rich history, with Franz Liszt and the Brahms brothers, Johannes and Friedrich, once headlining in the ballroom. Accessed via a clunking old-fashioned lift, the rooms in the Saski are decorated in period style and brimming with personality.

Senacki

Ul. Grodzka 51; tel: 012 422 76 86; www.hotelsenacki.pl; €€€

Positioned halfway between the Main Market Square and Wawel, the Senacki has 20 traditionally decorated, comfortable rooms with modern bathrooms, mostly with strong showers, a few with baths. The beamed ceiling and carved stone pillars in the ground-floor dining room demonstrate the 14th-century heritage of the building, while the café-bar shows its 13th-century origins. The young, friendly staff are knowledgeable and very helpful.

Stary

Ul. Szczepańska 5; tel: 012 384 08 08; www.stary.hotel.com.pl; €€€€

In a building that was for more than a century the home of wealthy Krakow industrialists, this gorgeous pile has been renovated into a sublime hotel that combines the medieval seamlessly with the latest conveniences. So while the rooms are wooden-floored and retain

The rooftop bar at Stary

their character – including original frescoes in some cases – the bathrooms are high-tech, all with Jacuzzis and marble tiling. Some rooms have small balconies with views to Main Market Square, there's a swimming pool in the cellar and a rooftop bar.

Wentzl

Rynek Główny 19; tel: 012 430 26 64; www.wentzl.pl; €€€

The Wentzl not only has views of the Main Market Square – it is right on it. Its rich colours and personal decor make it a home from home. Staff are friendly in a number of languages, and the service – as well as the location, of course – certainly makes up for the somewhat small and slightly overpriced rooms. The hotel has two upmarket restaurants, on the first floor and in the cellar, plus a ground-floor café that serves what locals insist is the best ice cream in the city.

Wit Stwosz

Ul. Mikołajska 28; tel: 012 429 60 26; www.wit-stwosz.com.pl; €€

A couple of minutes' walk from Main Market Square, this historic building dating from the 16th century has recently been renovated in traditional style. For what you are paying, it's a bargain, offering huge, comfortable beds and large windows that swamp the rooms with bags of lights. An atmospheric cellar restaurant serves great Polish and international food.

Around Wawel Hill

Benefis

Ul. Burska 2; tel: 012 252 01 71; www.hotelbenefis.pl; €€

While the onus at this three-star hotel is on functionality, the rooms are very smart, sharp and brightened with whimsical touches such as leaf-patterned duvets and dashes of modern art.

Copernicus

Ul. Kanonicza 16; tel: 012 424 34 00; www.copernicus.hotel.com.pl; €€€€

Hiding behind a deceptive Renaissance facade is a small modern hotel, with a pool and atrium courtyard, a short walk from Wawel Hill. The rooms may not all have Jacuzzis, but all are equally regal in their decor: woodcarvings and marble abound amid rich wallpaper and deep carpets. Service carries a personal touch. The hotel's (expensive) upmarket restaurant offers perhaps the most adventurous Polish food in the land. The outstanding dishes include appetisers such as wild boar ham stewed in dried fruits and mains such as pike perch served on parsley mousse with purple potatoes.

Novotel Krakow Centrum

Ul. Kościuszki 5; tel: 012 299 29 00; www.novotel.com; €€

Despite being part of a chain, this gem is a sound option for its array of free extras. It has a huge pool, the restaurants are excellent, and the rooms are

Some hotels' facilities include salt rooms for 'natural healing'

comfortable and cosy, even if rather corporate. From the upper floors there are great views of Wawel – these rooms come at no extra cost, so be sure to ask for one when you reserve.

Qubus Krakow

Ul. Nadwiślańska 6; tel: 012 374 51 00; www.qubushotel.com; €€

If the ultra-modern design isn't quite to your taste, then the views from the top-floor swimming pool over the old centre of Krakow certainly will be. Rooms are all well furnished, have lovely bathrooms, and the televisions must be among the biggest in the city. Good service and a reasonable rate make this a decent choice for bargainhunters. The hotel has a trendy, split-level piano bar – called After Work – which is a wonder of contemporary design and has a fine cocktail list.

Radisson Blu Hotel Krakow

Ul. Straszewskiego 17; tel: 012 618 88 88; www.radissonblu.com/hotel-krakow; €€€

Swedish-owned and operated luxury, where the rooms – decorated in pastel shades – are large, and the service is as fussy or as discreet as you want it to be. Bathrooms are a particular treat, with their heated floors, wide range of complimentary cosmetics and super-soft robes. There is an on-site sauna, good restaurants and a comfortable lobby bar. Surprisingly affordable for the high standard.

Sheraton Krakow

Ul. Powiśle 7; tel: 012 662 10 00; www.sheraton.pl/krakow; €€€

Well placed on the banks of the Vistula for both the Old Town and Wawel Castle, the Sheraton is a Krakow institution. Facilities include a pool. Even those who do not stay in its fine rooms – which pack a big punch in a small space – will often drop by to indulge themselves at one of the international-style restaurants and bars. The Someplace Else bar, with its television screen showing sports, is one of the most popular expatriate hang-outs in the whole of Poland; it's also, perhaps surprisingly, a fun place to take the kids. Meanwhile, The Olive, the Sheraton's classier dining option, is a sublime mix of modern service and decor and traditional Mediterranean food. How they manage to get fish and seafood this fresh so far from the sea is anyone's guess, but it explains the high prices.

Kazimierz

Abel

Ul. Józefa 30; tel: 012 411 87 36; www.hotelabel.pl; €

In the heart of the Kazimierz district, this historic hostel offers 14 immaculate and brightly coloured rooms for a great price. All rooms have en suite facilities, though note that some lack air conditioning, which is not ideal in Krakow in high summer. What we love best is the sparkling service from

A more traditional room

happy, smiling staff and the exquisite wooden staircase that leads up to the rooms.

Aparthotel Spatz

Ul. Miodowa 11; tel: 012 424 01 00;
www.pl.spatz.pl; €€

A stylish, minimalist hotel that makes use of plasma screens and a combination of cream and chocolate colours. Highly recommended, though at this price you may expect a greater range of facilities, such as maid service and air conditioning.

Astoria

Ul. Józefa 24; tel: 012 432 50 10;
http://astoriahotel.pl; €€

A spotless three-star jaunt decorated with a fuchsia facade and rooms in pink and brown. While the rather neutral design won't stir you to flights of fancy, the welcome at the front desk is warm and the location bang in the centre of Kazimierz.

Eden

Ul. Ciemna 15; tel: 012 430 65 65;
www.hoteleden.pl; €€

A carefully restored 15th-century building now opened as a hotel, in the heart of Kazimierz. It is aimed mainly at Jewish visitors with what we are led to believe is the only mikvah (Jewish ritual bath) in the country. There is a sauna, a health-giving salt cave and a delightful garden, too. Good value for money.

Ester

Ul. Szeroka 20; tel: 012 429 11 88;
www.hotel-ester.krakow.pl; €€

In the heart of Kazimierz, opposite the Old Synagogue museum, and within walking distance of Wawel Castle, the Ester's small scale (only 50 guests fit in when full) lends a personal touch, and staff are friendly. Rooms are well decorated in pleasant colours and the smart, contemporary-style restaurant serves Polish and Jewish cuisine. The hotel also has parking spaces and a cellar bar.

Karmel

Ul. Kupa 15; tel: 012 430 67 00;
www.karmel.com.pl; €€€

Lugging your luggage upstairs isn't much fun, and the rooms are something of a squash, but negatives aside, the Karmel is a bit of a treasure, with well-appointed quarters, pearly white designs and a side-street location on one of the area's quieter thoroughfares.

Kazimierz's Secret

Ul. Józefa 34; tel: 012 428 01 15;
www.kazimierzs-secret.com; €€

Ten-plus apartments, all recently completed to a high standard. With names including Bishop's Apartment and Lucky Number 13, the digs are nowhere near as imaginative as one envisages, but they still offer good-quality comfort as well as everything from washing machines to kitchens. A good option for families.

Klezmer-Hois

Ul. Berka Joselewicza 19; tel: 012 442 75 00; http://hotelmetropolitan.pl; €€
Located on the principal street of the Kazimierz district, near the Tempel and Remuh synagogues, this fin-de-siècle town-house hotel has a popular café and restaurant with live music. The rooms and apartments are large and clean, if a little basic (not all bathrooms are en suite), and they represent decent value for the price.

Metropolitan

Ul. Szeroka 6; tel: 012 411 12 45; www.klezmer.pl; €€€€
This gorgeous, upmarket boutique hotel in an elegant renovated 19th-century building opened in 2013 and is already acclaimed as one of the best places to stay in the city. As you would expect from a hotel of this standing, the rooms are tastefully decorated in contemporary style, the restaurant is top-notch (with excellent buffet breakfasts), the bar is super-cool, the gym is swanky, the service is exceptional, and the WiFi is free.

Around Planty

Andels

Ul. Pawia 3; tel: 012 660 01 00; www.vi-hotels.com/andels-cracow; €€
This modern hotel situated opposite the railway station is as lovely inside as it is ugly from the exterior. Interior design is the main draw here. The powerful reds, Cubist furniture and

cutting-edge technology in the rooms (think plasma television screens and sleek DVD players) plus competitive room rates suggest this place is more a business than tourist choice.

Ascot

Ul. Radziwiłłowska 3; tel: 012 384 06 66; www.ascothotel.pl; €€
Equidistant from the station and from Main Market Square, this modern hotel offers pretty standard rooms at a nevertheless decent price. The doubles are a little small, though the triples and family rooms are very well sized. All rooms have good bathrooms, air conditioning and a super-fast internet connection. Common areas are a bit dull, but the staff are helpfulness personified. Decent buffet breakfasts.

Europejski

Ul. Lubicz 5 (enter from ul. Radziwiłłowska); tel: 012 423 25 10; www.he.pl; €€
A few minutes' walk from the Planty gardens and Juliusz Słowacki Theatre, this period building offers flexible accommodation, including an attractive 'mansion-block apartment suite' at around the price of a double in a town centre hotel. There is a stylish bar, a good restaurant and parking.

Fortuna

Ul. Czapskich 5; tel: 012 411 08 06; www.hotel-fortuna.com.pl; €€
This newly renovated period building in a neighbourhood of eclectic late 19th-

Rustic Polish interior

century architecture contains a great little hotel with relatively cosy rooms and a nicely furnished restaurant/café. It also offers parking.

Greg & Tom Hostel

Ul. Pawia 12/7; tel: 012 422 41 00; http://gregtomhostel.com; €

Stags and hens are banned by Greg & Tom, and with dorms housing no more than six people it's odds on for a solid night's sleep. There's a real atmosphere of intimacy here, and, with six computers to share between a maximum of 23 guests, there are no queues to make a Skype call.

Holiday Inn

Ul. Wielopole 4–8; tel: 012 619 00 00; www.hik.krakow.pl; €€€

While lacking the cutting edge design dazzle of Krakow's newer hotels, the Holiday Inn remains a wise and popular choice. Amply proportioned rooms come with luxurious beds, soundproofed windows and a reserved style. Breakfast, conducted in the basement, gets full marks, while the location is just steps away from the Planty.

Ostoya Palace

U. Piłsudskiego 24; tel: 012 430 90 00; www.ostoyapalace.pl; €€

This very pretty hotel a few minutes' walk from the Main Market Square has been stylishly converted from a late 19th-century palace. The ambience is light and romantic, with parquet floors and traditional tiled stoves. Facilities include air conditioning. Note that most rooms have showers rather than baths. The cellar bar is a cosy cave to retreat into in bad weather. Some may find it a drawback that the restaurant is only open for breakfast and not in the evenings.

Pollera

Ul. Szpitalna 30; tel: 012 422 10 44; www.pollera.com.pl; €€

Beyond the classical facade, this hotel – situated opposite the Juliusz Słowacki Theatre and Holy Cross Church – offers delightful Secessionist interiors, including an exquisite floral stained-glass window on the staircase. Rooms are well sized and have antique furniture, lovely, relaxing beds as well as original wooden flooring. Note that some bathrooms have showers only (no tubs).

Polonia

Ul. Basztowa 25; tel: 012 422 12 33; www.hotel-polonia.com.pl; €€

Opened in 1917, this elegant, neoclassical hotel had a thorough refurbishment in 2007, which has really spruced it up. It's located right by a main traffic junction, but the thick double glazing ensures a peaceful night's sleep in all of the comfortable – if spartan – rooms. Well located for sightseeing, the hotel is directly opposite the Planty Gardens, and a few minutes from the main railway station.

Polski Pod Białm Orłem

Ul. Pijarska 17; tel: 012 422 11 44; www.podorlem.com.pl; €€€

This classical building next to the Czartoryski Museum and Florian's Gate, overlooking the original city walls, incorporates a very comfortable hotel. Though the rooms are a little bare, they are complemented by good bathrooms. The studios are well worth the extra, if you can afford it. Common areas are decorated with fine tapestries and reproductions of classic works of Polish art.

Pugetów

Ul. Starowiślna 15a; tel: 012 432 49 50; www.donimirski.com; €€€

A honeymoon experience set in a restored mansion house, the Pugetów is adorned with portraits of 19th-century damsels. Rooms in this romantic hideaway include fluffy bathrobes and locally sourced toiletries. While lacking in lifts, Pugetów redeems itself with oodles of character and obliging staff.

The Secret Garden Hostel

Ul. Skawińska 7; tel: 012 430 54 45; www.thesecretgarden.pl; €

The Secret Garden is a wonderful hostel in a city that has a good selection of them. This colourful place has comfortable dormitory-style rooms, as well as simple, immaculately clean private doubles, triples and quad rooms. Add in free WiFi, use of a washing machine, lockers and luggage storage, and you have the perfect backpacker stopover. And yes, it has a secret garden.

Wielopole

Ul. Wielopole 3; tel: 012 422 14 75; www.wielopole.pl; €€

Another bargain midway between the Old Town and Kazimierz, the Wielopole stands out for the polished attitude of the staff that can never do enough for you. The rooms are stylish, with simple showers, cable television and free internet in every room.

Krakow outskirts

Farmona Spa Hotel

Ul. Jugowicka 10c; tel: 012 252 70 70; www.farmonahotel.com; daily 7am–11pm; €

Situated a drive south of the city centre, the Farmona Spa Hotel is something of an oasis away from the bustle of the city. Surrounded by parkland, it has room for up to 60 guests, who can enjoy the hotel's range of wellness and beauty treatments, which all use natural products. The rooms and suites are decorated in modern, albeit slightly dated, style, but they offer very good value for money, given the price. The hotel's restaurant, the Magnifica, is a good addition to the Krakow restaurant scene and boasts of being child-friendly. Enjoy contemporary European and Asian dishes in hi-tech surroundings (the whole place is a WiFi hotspot and it's free), though you will need to book in advance if you want a table on the balcony during summer.

A twin room in traditional style

Nowa Huta

Santorini

Ul. Bulwarowa 35b; tel: 012 680 51 95;
www.santorinikrakow.pl; €€

If you've got a car or are interested in Nowa Huta, then this hotel offers very good value in a pleasant garden setting. Built in 2006, it has quiet mid-range rooms and a simple, homely style that makes use of muted browns. The in-house restaurant is by far the best place to eat in the area, offering surprisingly good, if simple, food.

Zakopane

Gospoda Pod Niebem

Ul. Droga Stanisława Zubka 5; tel: 018 206 29 09; www.podniebem.zakopane.pl; €

A charming wooden house on top of Gubałwka Hill. Expect little in the way of extras but prepare yourself for the invigorating smell of pine, more fresh air than you could ever wish for, and a fantastic view of the Tatras. For the price and location you can't really do better.

Grand Hotel Stamary

Ul. Kościuszki 19; tel: 018 202 45 10;
www.stamary.pl; €€€€

For the extra expense of staying here you get large rooms, decorated in fin-de-siècle style yet all featuring the latest in modern gadgets and conveniences. The service is exemplary from all of the immaculately attired staff. The Stamary also offers many facilities for families with children. Only the location (next to the resort's grotty bus station) lets it down a little, but once you're inside the hotel, you won't mind.

Litwor

Ul. Krupówki 40; tel: 018 202 42 00;
www.litwor.pl; €€€€

Located on a small square off Zakopane's main shopping promenade, this large, handsome hotel is one of the best places to stay in town. It has a delightful lobby bar, a great restaurant, nicely furnished rooms, an indoor swimming pool and fitness centre complete with sauna.

Sabała

Ul. Krupówki 11; tel: 018 201 50 92;
http://sabala.zakopane.pl; €€€

A giant chalet planted on Zakopane's busiest street, rooms come with log-cutter furnishings and warming winter extras such as heated bathroom flooring, while the sauna and pool are among the best in town. Noise from the live mountain bands that lurk the streets can be a problem.

Villa Marilor

Ul. Kościuszki 18; tel: 018 200 06 70;
www.hotelmarilor.pl; €€€

Located in a gorgeous 19th-century villa, this hotel makes good use of the huge rooms, with high ceilings and enormous pieces of furniture. Most of the rooms have large balconies, and a few have lovely mountain views: ask for one of these when you make a reservation.

Traditional Polish street food

RESTAURANTS

Eating out is one of the pleasures of visiting Krakow. There is a wealth of good restaurants in the city, and almost all have outside seating during the summer. While Polish cooking itself is tasty and filling enough to keep anyone happy for a short trip, the cosmopolitan nature of Krakow means that there is also a vast range of restaurants serving a variety of cuisines from all over the world. Particularly impressive are the Italian and sushi sectors. Even vegetarians – neglected in other parts of Eastern Europe – will have plenty to choose from (although watch out for the ubiquitous pork fat).

Not, surprisingly, the Old Town features the best choice of restaurants in the city, from stalls selling spicy lamb and falafel delicacies to ostentatious tourist traps with Western prices. It's the best place to try traditional fare in fairytale surroundings. Waiting staff in all but the most basic of city-centre restaurants speak English.

Be careful when paying in a Krakow restaurant: saying 'thank you' when

you hand over money to a waiter or waitress signifies that you do not require any change. Also note many of Krakow's restaurants close surprisingly early, and most take their last kitchen orders some time before the published closing time. Arriving at any restaurant much after 10pm will usually warrant shakes of the head and the words 'Kitchen's closed'.

Old Town

Alef

Ul. św Agnieski 5; tel: 012 424 31 31; www.alef.pl; daily 1–10pm; €€€
One of the city's most popular Jewish restaurants, Alef moved out of its spiritual home of Kazimierz to a street a little further north close to the Old Town, which gave it an outdoor eating space for summer. The furnishings of antiques and Jewish bits and bobs remains, and the food is still average, but Alef's main draw, however, is the excellent nightly live Jewish and Roma music that adds to the entire experience.

Aqua e Vino

Ul. Wiślna 5/10; tel: 012 421 25 676; www.aquaevino.pl; daily 1–10.30pm; €€€
A great Italian restaurant in a medieval cellar with attached lounge bar, run by an Italian. The minimalist decor

> Prices are for a two-course meal for two with a good bottle of wine:
> €€€€ = over 170zł
> €€€ = 100–170zł
> €€ = 50–100zł
> € = below 50zł

Polish pizzas

includes large black-and-white photographs of famous people eating Italian food. There's a fine wine list to accompany the food too.

Balaton

Ul. Grodzka 37; tel: 012 422 04 69;
www.balaton.krakow.pl; daily noon–10pm;
€€

Stuffed peppers and fiery goulashes are the mainstay of this veteran restaurant, which deserves particular praise in a city that prefers to pander to the timid Polish palate. In a certain light Balaton can appear tired and shabby, but that changes when the sun sets and Roma bands stroll between the candle-lit tables.

Bar 13

Rynek Główny 13; tel: 012 617 02 12;
Mon–Sat 9am–9pm, Sun 11am–5pm;
€€€€

This is one of the more upmarket cafés on the square, yet remains a good place to unwind while sightseeing around the Old Town. Coffee, tea, cocktails, cakes, sandwiches and huge salads all served at relatively expensive prices.

Bar Grodzki

Ul. Grodzka 47; tel: 012 422 68 07;
www.grodzkibar.zaprasza.net;
Mon–Sat 9am–7pm, Sun 10am–7pm;
€€

You'll find hearty Polish fare with plenty of shredded cabbage in a choice of halls, from the not exactly salubrious ground-floor canteen-looking space to the more upscale vaulted brick cellar below. The good-value food comes in gut-busting proportions guaranteed to keep visitors full for hours.

Café Camelot

Ul. św Tomasza 17; tel: 012 421 01 23;
daily 9am–midnight; €€

On a quiet corner a few steps from the city's main square, this busy ground-floor café serves lights meals, excellent salads and is famed for its apple cake.

La Campana

Ul. Kanonicza 7; tel: 012 423 22 32;
www.lacampana.pl; daily noon–11pm;
€€€

This charming Italian restaurant is housed in the lovely House Under Three Crowns. It's all you would expect from an authentic Italian, with good pastas and risottos, as well as fish and meat dishes. There is a pleasant garden for summer dining.

Chłopskie Jadło

Ul. św Jana 3; tel: 725 100 535;
www.chlopskiejadlo.pl; daily noon–11pm;
€€€

The Peasant's Kitchen evokes the traditional spirit of Polish-style hospitality in a wonderful replica of a 19th-century country inn. Fine country cooking includes the likes of *bigos* (hunter's stew, comprising five different types of meat simmered with mushrooms, cabbage and sauerkraut) and *golonka* (pork

cooked in beer), served with mustard and horseradish.

CK Dezerter

Ul. Bracka 6; tel: 012 422 79 31; www.ckdezerter.pl; Mon–Fri 9am–11pm, Sat–Sun 9am–midnight; €€€

With dishes from all over Central Europe on offer (recommended is the *bograzsgulas*, a Hungarian goulash cooked very slowly in a kettle suspended over an open fire), you are bound to find something here you like. There is a surprisingly good choice for vegetarians, and though the place itself is a little gloomy inside, it is homely and a haunt of both locals and visitors.

Cyklop

Ul. Mikołajska 16; tel: 012 421 66 03; www.pizzeriacyklop.pl; daily 11am–11pm; €€

This is a friendly place with simple decor. It enjoys a reputation for serving the city's best pizza, which is cooked in a traditional, wood-fired oven. It is deservedly popular, so expect to queue during peak hours or even share a table; no reservations.

Cyrano de Bergerac

Ul. Sławkowska 26; tel: 012 411 72 88; www.cyranodebergerac.pl; daily noon–11pm; €€€€

A regular and proud winner of the *Best Restaurant in Galicia (Lesser Poland)* award. This achievement might not sound like a big deal in a region not known for the quality of its dining establishments, but Cyrano de Bergerac would be a contender whatever the locale or standard of competition. This is opulent dining in the extreme, with prices to match. The fillet steak is excellent, as are the Polish highlights, such as *pierogi* (Polish dumplings – small dough parcels filled with anything from minced pork or beef to cabbage and potato or sweet berries). A superb list of French wines befits the superior wine cellar setting of high ceilings and antique furniture. There is also a delightful courtyard garden for alfresco dining in the summer months.

Da Pietro

Rynek Główny 17; tel: 012 422 32 79; www.dapietro.pl; daily 12.30pm–midnight; €€€€

This spacious and elegant cellar restaurant has professional, attentive staff and an engaging 'smart-casual' atmosphere. It has a deserved reputation for reliable, enjoyable Italian food, comprising all that country's classic dishes, including some of the best pork steaks in Poland and a sensational *bistecca fiorentina*. It is no wonder that people keep coming back for more. You can have a cheaper option of pizza or pasta.

La Fontaine

Ul. Slawkowska 1; tel: 012 422 65 64;

Szara's dining room

www.lafontaine-restaurant.pl; daily noon–11pm; €€€

Francophiles convene at La Fontaine, a labyrinthine venue occupying a 13th-century cellar. Adding class to Krakow's culinary chart is the up-and-coming French chef, with morel mushrooms and foie gras part of his perfectly formed repertoire. Choose from traditional French onion soup or more innovative dishes such as French young pork served three ways. Try and get a courtyard table.

Gehanowska Restauracja Pod Słońcem

Rynek Główny 43; tel: 012 422 93 78 ext.17; www.gehanowska.pl; daily 8am–midnight; €€€

A classy, august venue with plenty of wood panelling, oil paintings and delicate crockery: the ground-floor café is principally aimed at a pensioned and prosperous crowd, while the vaulted cellar restaurant serves some of the more unusual traditional Polish dishes such as knuckle of pork in beer.

Green Way

Ul. Krupnicza 22; no phone, email: Krakow@greenway.pl; www.greenway.pl; daily 9am–9pm; €€

Poland's number one vegetarian restaurant, part of a nationwide chain, sees bespectacled students and old ladies jostle at the counter over some of the best non-meat-based dishes in town. The dishes here are enormous and good value. A tough one to beat.

Guliwer

Ul. Bracka 6; tel: 012 430 24 66; www.guliwer-restauracja.pl; daily 9am–11; €€€

Proud of its wine list featuring many French names, this relaxed and popular café-bar is a good place to take a break from sightseeing. As well as soups, salads and fish, there is a different hotpot every day, such as *chulent*, *choucroute* or *makluba*. There are some tasty desserts too, such as traditional Polish apple cake and homemade cheesecake with raspberry sauce.

łkałkaHawełka

Rynek Główny 34 (ground floor); tel: 012 422 06 31; www.hawelka.pl; daily 11am–11pm; €€€

Still the first choice for those looking for a formal dining venue, this place long ago lost its crown as the city's best eatery. That said, the food remains very good – if a tad expensive – and the service as stuffy and fussy as you would expect. For a splurge it takes some beating.

Indus Tandoor

Ul. Sławkowska 13–15; tel: 012 423 22 82; www.indus.pl; Sun–Thu noon–10pm, Fri–Sat noon–midnight; €€€

Photographs of India's most sumptuous palaces line the walls of one of Krakow's finest Indian restaurants. Poles have yet to really take to Indian food, so expect a solely foreign clientele, and dishes that will not be as hot

The traditional U Babci Maliny

as you might normally expect. Ask the waiter nicely, however, and he will ask the chef to spice things up for you.

Kawaleria

Ul. Golbia 4; tel: 012 430 24 32; www.kawaleria.com.pl; daily noon–10pm; €€€€

This is a special night out: the cooking wins awards and the surroundings and service are dashing. The menu is Polish with a modern slant, changing with the seasons, and often features wild boar or venison. There's a romantic garden for summer dining.

Leonardo

Ul. Szpitalna 20/22; tel: 012 429 68 50; www.leonardo.com.pl; daily 11am–11pm; €€€

Dine in the Leonardo Salon, adorned with da Vinci's scientific designs, or in the Wine Chamber, with rough-hewn walls and country kitchen-style trappings. There is a choice of Polish or Italian menu, with the Polish chef trained by renowned Italian, Alfredo Chrochetti. All the regions of Italy are well represented and dishes range from traditional pasta to innovative meat and fish dishes.

Miod Malina

Ul. Grodzka 40; tel: 012 430 04 11; www.miodmalina.pl; daily noon–11pm; €€€

With one of the most welcoming hearths in Poland, this lovely little restaurant is packed out most nights, so book ahead. The food is good, based on the cuisine of Małopolska (Lesser Poland), with plenty of game.

Miód Wino

Ul. Slawkowska 32; tel: 012 422 74 95; www.miodiwino.pl; daily 11am–11pm; €€€

A good choice to fill hungry faces amidst suits of armour and stuffed animal heads, this medieval-feel favourite comes complete with waiting staff in traditional costumes and an extensive menu to leave all but the most ravenous feeling satisfied. Try the classic *żurek* soup, a national classic made from fermented rye flour.

Padre

Ul. Wiślna 11; tel: 012 430 62 99; www.restauracja-padre.pl; daily Mon–Sat 11am–10pm, Sun noon–9pm; €€

Padre has a charming terrace during the summer and a gorgeous, unpretentious cellar restaurant for the colder months. The menu is described as 'flavours of the world', with a slant towards Italian and Indian cuisines. The waitresses are pleasant enough, and the piped music is always entertaining.

Paese

Ul. Poselska 24; tel: 012 421 62 73; www.paese.com.pl; Mon–Fri 1–11pm; €€€

Attempting to recreate a Corsican village feel in Poland is bound to miss the mark, but that's no reason to give this

Polish pastries

boat-themed restaurant a wide berth. Both the food and the service are outstanding (visiting groups should try one of the marvellous fondues), and its location, cunningly hidden in one of the Old Town's lesser-known back streets, tends to keep the hordes away.

Szara

Rynek Główny 6 (corner ul. Sienna); tel: 012 421 66 69; www.szara.pl; daily 11am–11pm; €€€€

Understated, discreet, but excellent, Szara is now a mainstay of the Main Market Square, and an essential part of a trip to Krakow. Don't panic if you can't bag an outside table: inside is a treat, with beautifully painted vaulted ceilings and large tables only adding to the joy of dining here. The food lives up to its surroundings, with delicious dishes like reindeer tartare and Provençale snails, all rather cutting-edge for Polish cuisine.

Taco Mexicano Cuatro Elementos

Rynek Główny 19; tel: 012 429 52 99; www.tacomexicano.pl; Sun–Mon noon–10pm, Tue–Wed noon–10.30pm, Thu noon–11pm, Fri–Sat noon–midnight; €€€

The stone cellar interior of this taco and tapas bar is a nice enough place to eat, and the food is surprisingly good. This is a spicy and refreshing change from the Polish/European restaurants that otherwise have a monopoly on the Old Town. The nachos are tasty, though the portions are small, and the main courses are better value: try the *chihuahua burritos*.

Trattoria Soprano

Ul. św. Anny 7; tel: 012 422 51 95; www.trattoriasoprano.pl; daily 10am–midnight; €€

Krakow is full of sub-standard Italian restaurants; this is an exception. You will find good, simple Italian food, such as *papardelle* with salmon and mascarpone, at reasonable prices. The setting is pleasant: a spacious room decorated in Mediterranean shades.

U Babci Maliny

Ul. Sławkowska 17; tel: 012 422 76 01; www.kuchniaubabcimaliny.pl; daily 11am–9pm; €

In keeping with its name ('At Your Granny Malina's'), this eatery (hidden away towards the back of an unpromising academic building) serves up dishes typically cooked by a Polish granny. It's all great value and so popular that another branch has opened in Krakow at ul. Szpitalna 38. Classic peasant food – fermented rye soup with potatoes and sausage, *grochówka z grzankami* (pea soup with croutons), *placki ziemniaczane* (grated potato pancakes) – is served in generous quantities. It's self-service: order at the counter and pick up a number, which flashes on a small screen when your meal is ready. Collect the food yourself, and – de

Terrace service at Wentzl

rigueur for Krakow self-service – take your plates to the hatch when you've finished.

Wesele

Rynek Główny; tel: 012 422 74 60; www.weselerestauracja.pl; daily 10am–11pm; €€€

Even in a square lauded for its restaurants, Wesele stands out as something special. Rustic interiors feature plenty of flowers and carpentry, while the food scores highly for fantastic translations of local dishes. The goose is a highlight, although those wishing to sample it might want to book a table ahead. The roe deer marinated in red wine, goes down a treat, too.

Wentzl

Rynek Główny 19; tel: 012 429 52 99; www.restauracjawentzl.com.pl; daily 1pm–11pm; €€€€

A true Krakow legend, with a restaurant pedigree going all the way back to 1792, Wentzl offers a classic and Polish menu that is extended by a number of Viennese specialities, especially desserts. Given its imposing pavement facade and the ground-floor café's icing-sugar colour scheme, the 'fine-dining' restaurant rooms located in the cellar and on the first floor are something of a surprise, as is the quality of the fresh Hungarian foie gras. The unique decor is best described as a meeting of vaulted antiquity with postmodern metalwork sculptures.

Wierzynek

Rynek Główny 15; tel: 012 424 96 00; www.wierzynek.com.pl; daily 1pm–11pm; €€€€

Older than any other restaurant in the city, this place can trace its history back to a banquet served here in 1364. It occupies two Renaissance houses, and there is a selection of elegant, antique-furnished dining rooms where quality Polish dishes are served. For a less formal meal, try the grill room in the basement.

Zapiecek

Ul. Sławkowska 32, tel: 012 422 74 95; www.zapiecek.eu; open 24 hours a day; €

Local speciality *pierogi* (a kind of Polish dumpling) stuffed with a seemingly endless variety of favourite fillings are served here. Order and pay for what you want from the counter, then move along and pick up your food from the hatch. If you don't like disposable plates, this is not the place for you.

Zen

Ul. św Tomasza 29; tel: 012 426 55 55; www.zensushi.pl; daily noon–midnight; €€€

On the ground floor, visitors snap up sushi sets as they float by on boats, while upstairs it's shoes off and legs crossed as diners sit in proper Japanese style on mats and cushions. The raw fish is highly rated, but for the real gourmet experience prepare to spend big for the hand-massaged Kobe beef.

Kazimierz

Al Dente

Ul. Kupa 12; tel: 012 430 04 18;
www.aldentekrakow.pl; daily noon–11pm;
€€€

Al Dente's chief claim to fame is the largest choice of pasta in Krakow, and you'll find many locals professing this to be their favourite Italian in town. The team specialises in the cuisine of Sardinia, served in an urbane, ice-white dining room completing a memorable experience.

Alrina Restaurant

Bulwar Kurlandzki (at the top of ul. Gazowej, near Kładka Bernatka);
tel: 066 882 04 54; www.alrina.pl;
Mon–Fri noon–10pm, Sat–Sun noon–midnight; €€€€

It's difficult to surprise the cool hipsters of Kazimierz, but this new arrival has generated a lot of praise. This restaurant on a Dutch barge, has dining on deck in summer and a smart modern interior with a separate bar area for less fine days. The seasonal menu treats traditional Polish ingredients, including sheep's cheese, venison and berries, in a modern way, and there is a simple children's menu.

Ariel

Ul. Szeroka 18; tel: 012 421 79 20;
www.ariel.krakow.pl; daily 10am–midnight;
€€€€

Choose from pavement tables, a sheltered courtyard with a goldfish pond, or the conservative, 1970s-style dining room with paintings depicting Jewish life. There's plenty of choice on the Polish/Jewish menu, with classics such as herring fillets in sour cream, fried *kreplah* and carp sautéed with onions and mushrooms. The second-floor room has live music nightly. A small bookshop in the entrance hall sells guidebooks and souvenirs from Kazimierz.

Bagelmama

Ul. Dajwór 10; tel: 012 346 16 46;
www.bagelmama.com; daily 9am–6pm;
€

The best thing ever to happen to lunchtime in Krakow, this place brings a little piece of New York to Kazimierz. Bagelmama has a few tables for those who don't want to takeaway. Every kind of bagel you can think of has a range of toppings: sweet or savoury. Or chose from their list of tapas, wraps, soups, salads and desserts. The coffee is very good, too.

Cafe Młynek

Plac Wolnica 7; tel: 012 430 62 02;
www.cafemlynek.com; daily 8am–midnight;
€€

With art exhibitions, breakfast concerts, poetry and the odd 'raving party' of dance music, this place adds liveliness to its vegetarian offering. The food, from potato pancakes to pasta dishes, is simple and inexpensive; to drink there's beer on draught or choose from a very short wine list.

A good selection of wines at Szara

Dawno Temu na Kazimierzu

Ul. Szeroka 1; tel: 012 421 21 17; daily 10am–10.30pm; €€€

This terrific little restaurant is disguised to look like a row of early 20th-century traders' shops and is topped with awnings relating Kazimierz's Jewish past. Inside it is a riot of antiques – all bought or found in the area – with an enjoyable clutter that is hard to dislike. The food is pretty standard Jewish fare; though note that the restaurant is not kosher.

Deli Bar

Ul. Meisels 5; tel: 012 430 64 04; www.delibar.pl; Tue–Thu 1–10pm, Fri–11pm, Sat–Sun noon–11pm; €€

A pleasant minimalist feel with the added bonus of a good summer terrace, Hungarian food never tasted this good, at least not in Poland. In addition to a knockout spicy goulash, among the other excellent-value dishes here are some great salads, soups and even a decent selection of wine.

Kuchnia u Doroty

Ul. Augustiańska 4; tel: 051 794 53 38; daily 10am–9pm; €

This simple place is popular for its low prices and straightforward approach to food. Visit to refuel on good homemade Polish fare but don't expect the lace doilies or bohemian atmosphere you'll find elsewhere in Kazimierz.

Momo

Ul. Dietla 49; tel: 609 68 57 75; daily 11am–8pm; €

Famous throughout Poland, this small and assuming wholefood and vegetarian restaurant between the Old Town and Kazimierz provides good healthy food, from brown rice dishes to a range of excellent salads. Don't be put off by the canteen appearance – there are some truly appetising dishes on offer here, representing excellent value. Cash only, no cards.

Polakowski

Ul. Miodowa 39; tel: 012 421 21 17; www.polakowski.com.pl; daily 9am–10pm; €

Grab a tray, join the queue, then scoop out meat and vegetables from steaming-hot containers before settling down with low-cost diners eating the local way. Operating since 1899, the *bigos* here is as legendary as the venue. Distinguishing Polakowski from the classic milk-bar experience are an English menu, countryside decorations and a toilet that flushes.

Rubinstein

Ul. Szeroka 12 (Rubinstein Hotel); tel: 012 384 00 00; www.rubinstein.pl; open daily from noon–10pm; €€€€

Situated on the ground floor of the hotel of the same name, this restaurant is a sumptuous place where the waiters are immaculately dressed in dinner jackets and guests are expected to be at least reasonably smartly attired. There is a good number of fish dishes

The wonderfully named Dawno Temu na Kazimierzu (Once Upon a Time in Kazimier)

on the menu here – something of a rarity in Krakow – though such luxuries come at a high price. The wine list is short but excellent. The elegant hotel is named after the cosmetics icon Helena Rubinstein, who was born on this street. It has 22 mostly spacious, traditionally decorated rooms and five large, lavish suites, all of which are spread over seven floors.

Szara Kazimierz
Ul. Szeroka 39; tel: 012 429 12 19; www.szarakazimierz.pl; daily 11am–11pm; €€€€

A mainstay of Main Market Square, Szara's Kazimierz branch offers something different from the standard Jewish fare of the area, with an interesting menu of modern European food and some sensational fusion dishes that combine seafood and traditional Polish cuisine. Other pluses include the polite staff and the decent – though not cheap – prices.

Krakow outskirts

Villa Decius
Ul. 28 Lipca 17a; tel: 012 425 33 90; www.vd-restauracja.pl; daily 1pm–10pm; €€€€

It's a bit of a trek to reach this eatery from the centre of town, and it is off the scale price-wise, but it's certainly worth the effort and expense to dine on well-prepared Italian, Polish and other European dishes within the palatial Italianate Renaissance Villa Decius;

the grand restored building is a feast in itself. Finely attired waiters make you feel very special as they whisk away huge silver domes to reveal beautifully crafted food, such as the foie gras lightly sautéed in vintage champagne.

Szara Kazimierz

NIGHTLIFE

Should you feel like dancing, going to a concert or the theatre, Krakow can oblige. The local listings guide *Krakow In Your Pocket* (www.inyourpocket.com/poland/krakow) will tell you where's hot.

Theatre and Cabaret

Juliusz Słowacki Theatre
pl. Świętego Ducha 1;
tel: 021 424 45 00; www.slowacki.krakow.pl
Grand edifice staging Polish and foreign classic and contemporary drama.

Narodowy Stary Teatr
Ul. Jagiellonska 1; tel: 012 422 90 80; www.stary.pl
Though performances are usually in Polish, there are times during the year when local cultural centres sponsor performances in other languages.

Music

Harris Piano Jazz Bar
Rynek Główny 28; tel: 012 421 57 41; www.harris.krakow.pl
An archetypal cool jazz bar that does great drinks at very reasonable prices.

Jazz Club u Muniaka
Ul. Florianska 3; tel: 012 423 12 05
One of Krakow's most legendary jazz clubs at the bottom of a flight of stairs in a 14th-century cellar. Great acoustics and an intimate atmosphere.

Opera Krakowska
Ul. Lubicz 48; tel: 012 296 62 62; www.opera.krakow.pl
The Opera Krakowska has existed since the late 19th century, but lacked its own performance space until 2008 when it moved into a brand-new building that seats 720 people and features outstanding acoustics.

Piwnica pod Baranami
Rynek Glowny 27; tel: 012 421 25 00/012 423 07 68
Home to the annual Krakow Jazz Festival among other things, the basement of this former old palace is the best place in town to watch cabaret and listen to jazz.

Szymanowski Philharmonic
Ul. Zwierzyniecka 1; tel: 012 619 87 22; www.filharmonia.krakow.pl
You can enjoy Szymanowski Philharmonic performances most nights of the week, with matinée concerts on Sundays.

Bars and Clubs

Alchemia
Ul. Estery 5; tel: 012 421 22 00; www.alchemia.com.pl
A true bastion of Kazimierz cool, this venue has been attracting playwrights and artists since its inception in 1999. Scruffy antiques and faded photographs often go unnoticed thanks to the near-Stygian blackness.

Intimate jazz club

Baccarat

Ul. Stolarska 13; tel: 0695 116 760;
www.baccaratclub.pl

Krakow's swankiest dance den is dripping with chandeliers and glittery trimmings. The ruthless door policy rewards the decadent.

Baroque

Ul. Św. Jana 16; tel: 012 422 01 06;
www.baroque.com.pl

Small and dark, this luxurious-looking restaurant-cum-bar wins prizes for a cool atmosphere. Some of the best drinks in the city, including a selection of over 100 vodkas, add local flavour to your evening.

Cień

Ul. Św. Jana 15; tel: 012 422 21 77;
www.cienklub.com

Rated by many as the best club in town, the lengthy line at the door reflects this. Look your best to make it past the door, before joining Krakow's other glamorous people in a blue-lit basement that specialises in house sounds.

CK Browar

Ul. Podwale 6/7; tel: 012 429 25 05;
www.ckbrowar.krakow.pl

Krakow's microbrewery attracts every social type, from track-suited teens to foreign beer enthusiasts, with a cellar location and sports broadcasts.

Movida

Ul. Mikołajska 9; tel: 012 429 45 97;
www.movida-bar.pl

A long, narrow space plastered with candid pictures of celebrities practising their pouts, Movida is one of the classiest places in town with cocktails that blow the competition sideways.

Taawa

Ul. Estery 18; tel: 012 421 06 00;
www.taawa.pl

Marking the area's merger with the mainstream is the opening of Taawa, a glitzy club with zappy laser lights and flock-style wallpaper patterns etched onto glass. Here it's all back-lit bars and plush furnishings, and a strict entry policy ensures most never make it past the velvet rope.

Cinema

ARS

Ul. Św. Jana 6; tel: 012 421 41 99;
www.ars.pl

An Old Town favourite catering predominantly, but not exclusively, to mainstream tastes.

Cinema City

Ul. Podgórska 34; tel: 012 254 54 00;
www.cinema-city.pl

Modern multiplex inside Galeria Kazimierz. Screens big Hollywood films.

Orange IMAX

Al. Pokoju 44; tel: 012 290 90 90;
www.kinoimax.pl

Allegedly the biggest screen in Europe, this is the place to come for the ultimate IMAX experience.

Wawel Cathedral

A–Z

A

Addresses

In Poland, the street name is written first, followed by the house or building number. Streets are usually numbered odd on one side, even on the other, though in many parts of Old Krakow, rather more arbitrary systems are used.

B

Business hours

Banks open early, usually at 8am, and stay open until about 6pm. All banks are closed at weekends. During the week, shops open at 9am or 10am and stay open until about 7pm, with shorter hours on Saturdays; many are closed on Sundays. Exceptions include shops inside big shopping malls, and markets; the latter are open by 5am and generally stay open until the middle of the afternoon. Museums and galleries generally open at 10am, and close any time from 2pm to 6pm. Most museums are closed on Mondays.

C

Climate

Winters are crisp and snowy, with December and January typically cold, damp and foggy. However, Krakow looks magnifi-cent in the snow, and the surrounding attractions, such as Zakopane, Poland's premier ski resort, are in full swing. Summers are usually hot and sunny from May to September, though September and October can be very wet. During the winter a warm coat, hat and gloves are required; even during the summer a light raincoat is advised.

Crime and safety

Although Krakow is generally safe, all cities pose a potential threat, so take sensible precautions. Don't leave coats hanging around with valuables in the pockets, or leave your mobile phone on a table. Take care when travelling on busy trams and in any crowded space, especially outdoor concerts. As in any city of this size, exercise caution when walking around late at night. Stick to well-lit streets, and if in doubt, use a taxi. Areas to be avoided late at night include the main railway station, the Planty gardens and ul. Westerplatte.

Customs regulations

Since Poland joined the EU in 2004, duty-free allowances no longer apply to travellers arriving from or leaving for other EU countries. However, some EU countries have imposed their own limits on what can be imported from Poland: the UK, for example, limits cigarette imports to 800.

All dressed up for Easter   *Horse-drawn carriage on Market Square*

Dogs and cats may be brought into the country, providing they are micro-chipped or tattooed, have a pet pass-port and certificates for the correct vaccinations from a vet who should check current regulations with the Pol-ish embassy in your own country.

Most Polish antiques and art-works that are not registered and not more than 50 years old can be freely exported. If permission is needed, you can apply at the Wojewódzki Urząd Ochrony Zabytków (ul. Kanonicza 24, necessary forms at www.wuoz.malo polska.pl) but a good antique dealer will take care of the paperwork for you. This can take a few months and may involve extra taxes.

D

Disabled travellers

All new buildings and building reno-vation work in Poland must meet rigid EU standards concerning the provision of facilities for the disabled. Places in Krakow such as the airport, many hotels and quite a few restaurants are now up to good European standards, despite the difficulty of reconciling the preser-vation of the Unesco-listed heritage of a medieval city with the needs of wheel-chair users.

Though more recently opened hotels have shown the way by providing wheel-chair facilities in 14th-century build-ings, Krakow's cobbled streets and many of its best sights remain hard

work for wheelchair users and travellers with other disabilities.

Wheelchair users can get around the city fairly easily on most forms of pub-lic transport. All new 'bendy' buses are designed for wheelchairs, as are the new-style trams which are being intro-duced across the network.

At Galeria Stańczyk (ul. Królewska 94; tel: 012 636 85 84; Mon–Fri 11am–5pm), a cultural centre for the disabled.

E

Electricity

Electricity is 220v AC, 50 Hz. Sockets are round with two-pins. Those from the UK, US and outside Continen-tal Europe need an adaptor. US and non-European visitors whose coun-tries use a 110v system need a voltage converter, though they are not neces-sary for most mobile phone and laptop chargers.

Embassies and consulates

Consulates (in Krakow)
US: ul. Stolarska 9; tel: 012 424 51 00; http://krakow.usconsulate.gov

Embassies (in Warsaw)
Australia: ul. Nowogrodzka 11; tel: 022 521 34 44; www.australia.pl.
Canada: ul. Matejki 1/5; tel: 022 584 31 00; www.canada.pl.
New Zealand: al. Ujazdowskie 51; tel: 022 521 05 00; www.nzembassy.com/poland.

Pharmacy sign

Republic of Ireland: ul. Mysia 5; tel: 022 849 66 33; www.irlandia.pl.

South Africa: ul. Koszykowa 54; tel: 022 622 10 31; www.southafrica.pl.

UK: ul Kawalerii 12, tel: 022 311 00 00; www.gov.uk/government/world/poland

Emergency numbers

In an emergency, call 999 for an ambulance, 997 for police or 998 for the fire brigade. From a mobile phone call 112 for general emergencies.

SOS for Foreigners: tel: 022 278 77 77 – receive professional advice from foreign language-speaking consultants: English, German and Russian.

G

Gay and lesbian travellers

Catholic Poland is a largely conservative country when it comes to social mores, with a far-from-enlightened attitude to members of its gay community.

That said, Krakow's city authorities have in recent years been more open to the gay community than those in the rest of the country. In fact, in the 2011 parliamentary elections, the liberal Palikot Movement's Anna Grodzka polled a large number of votes and became Europe's first transgendered MP.

The age of consent for homosexuals, as well as heterosexuals, is 15. Handy gay information to the city can be found at http://cracow.gayguide.net

H

Health

EU nationals: UK and EU citizens with a valid European Health Insurance Card (EHIC; available from post offices or online at www.ehic.org.uk in the UK) can receive free treatment, although private medical insurance is recommended. State health care in Poland is under-funded and poor. Bear in mind that salaries for state medical staff are low, and that 'gifts' are common and often necessary.

North Americans: You will need to take out medical insurance before travelling. While emergency treatment is technically free, all other services must be paid for.

Centrum Medicover (tel: 19677; www.medicover.com) operates a network of medical centres in Poland's major cities, including Krakow. It has English-speaking staff, a broad range of specialists and an ambulance service. Its programme includes home visits, and it will treat non-members. Medical services are also provided by Falck (tel: 19675; www.falck.pl) and Scanmed (tel: 012 629 88 00; www.scanmed.pl).

Dentists: Dentists who speak foreign languages can be booked at the private clinic Dental America, pl. Szczepański 3 (tel: 012 421 89 48; www.dentamerica. pl), and Dentamed, ul. Na Zjeździe 13 (tel: 012 259 80 00; www.denta-med. com.pl).

Catching up on the news

Pharmacies: There are several pharmacies (Apteka) offering a 24-hour service throughout the city, including those at ul. Galla 26 and ul. Karmelicka 23. For more information on all-night pharmacies, see www.apteki.lekarze.krakow.pl.

Water: The local tap water is safe to drink, though bottled water tastes better.

I

Internet

There are many inexpensive internet cafés in the centre, such as the 24-hour Hetmańska (ul. Bracka 4), but they are fast becoming redundant, as practically every café and restaurant offers WiFi to customers with laptops and smartphones. Look out, too, for the hotspot Cracovia logo signalling free WiFi at hotels and cafés.

M

Maps

Free city maps can be picked up in tourist information centres, hotels, bars, restaurants and cafés. A good map of Krakow is Compass's 1:50,000 scale edition, which covers the city in detail, lists public transport routes and has the only decent map of Nowa Huta in print.

Media

Newspapers: Polish broadsheets include *Dziennik Polski* (Polish Daily) and *Gazeta Wyborcza* (The Electorate's Newspaper). The free official listings magazine, *Karnet Krakow* (www.karnet.krakow.pl), has an English language section, while *Krakow In Your Pocket* (www.inyourpocket.com/poland/krakow) is an entertaining alternative. Both are monthly and widely available from newsagent kiosks, hotels and Empik outlets, as is the English-language monthly newspaper *Krakow Post* (www.krakowpost.com), which is good for local news.

Television: Most hotels have satellite TV offering English-language stations such as CNN and BBC World.

Radio: Local radio stations include Radio Krakow (www.radiokrakow.pl) on 101.6 FM, and Jazz Radio 101 FM. Polskie Radio's Polish news in English (www.thenews.pl) is available as a podcast or smartphone app.

Money

Currency: Poland's currency comprises złoty (paper notes and coins) and groszy (coins): 100 groszy equal 1 złoty. Groszy coins come in denominations of 1, 2, 5, 10, 20 and 50. Smaller denominations of złoty (1, 2 and 5 złoty) are coins; higher denominations (10, 20, 50, 100 and 200 złoty) are in the form of paper notes.

Bureaux de change: The best place to change money is in a bank, and there are many in the city centre, all offering similar exchange rates. While exchange kiosks and counters (marked Kantor) throughout the city offer better rates, they also

St Joseph's opulent interior

apply large commission charges. Beware signs declaring 'No Commission': these usually apply only when Polish currency is being sold.

Cash machines: Cash machines (ATMs) are the easiest way to get local currency. You'll find one at the Unicredit-Pekao Bank (Rynek Główny 31), at numerous sites in the square (nos 20 and 41) and at ul. Floriańska 6.

Credit cards: Internationally established credit cards, including American Express, Visa and MasterCard, are accepted by numerous hotels, restaurants and shops. Don't expect smaller establishments to accept credit cards, particularly not for small sums.

Cash advances on credit cards can be arranged at a number of banks, including Unicredit-Pekao, Rynek Główny 31. Bring your passport.

P

Post

Post offices: The post office near the main railway and bus stations, at ul. Lubicz 4 (tel: 012 422 91 68) offers a round-the-clock daily postal service for stamps, letters, money transfers and fax. Hours for its other services are Mon–Fri 7am–8pm, Sat 2pm–8pm, closed Sun. The post office at ul. Westerplatte 20 (tel: 012 421 03 48) is open Mon–Fri 8am–8pm, Sat 8am–2pm, but closed on Sun.

Stamps for postcards and letters abroad cost 2.40zł, or 1.55zł if you're

sending them within Poland. Red post boxes have a logo of a yellow post horn in a blue oval.

Public holidays

1 January New Year's Day
6 January Epiphany
March/April Easter Sunday and Easter Monday
1 May Labour Day
3 May Constitution Day
May/June Pentecost (7th Sunday after Easter)
June Corpus Christi (9th Thursday after Easter)
15 August Feast of the Assumption
1 November All Saints' Day
11 November Independence Day
25 December Christmas Day
26 December St Stephen's Day

R

Religion

Most Poles are Roman Catholic. Mass is said in English at 10.30am on Sundays at Kościół św Idziego (St Giles, on ul. Grodzka towards Wawel).

Though less common, Krakow also has churches and houses of worship for other denominations and faiths. These include Kościół św Marcina (Church of St Martin, Lutheran Congregation) on ul. Grodzka 58, Baptystów (Baptist church) on ul. Wyspiańskiego 4 and the Methodist Church on ul. Długa 3. Kazimierz's Remuh Synagogue (on ul. Szeroka 40) is the only

Krakow smiles   *Town Hall Tower clock*

synagogue where Friday and Saturday services are held regularly.

T

Telephones

Phone numbers: To call Krakow from outside the country, dial your international access code followed by 48 for Poland and the subscriber number minus the initial 0.

If you're calling a Krakow landline from anywhere in Poland, dial the 10-digit number beginning with 012. The same applies for calling a landline from a Polish mobile with the exception of Plus GSM, which requires the dropping of the first 0.

To get a line out of Poland, dial 00 plus whatever you need after that for the country in question (Australia 61, UK 44, US and Canada 1).

For directory enquiries in English when in Krakow, telephone 118 811.

Mobile phones: In order to avoid roaming costs it is recommended that you purchase a local prepaid SIM card. Several companies now offer extremely cheap start-up packages for less than 10zł, with top-up cards costing 5zł and upwards. Both are widely available and can be bought from several shops and kiosks dotted around the city as well as the airport, and bus and railway stations.

Time zones

Polish time is one hour ahead of GMT.

Tipping

It is customary to tip restaurant staff, taxi drivers and hotel porters about 10–15 percent.

Note that when paying in a restaurant, if you say 'thank you' when handing over the money the waiter will assume that he may keep the change. To make sure you get your change back say '*prosze*' as you hand over the money.

Toilets

In recent years, Krakow has been working on improving the public toilets in the city. There are now several with disabled access such as where ul.św.Tomasza meets the Planty. But, whether it's a public convenience, or in a café or restaurant, vigilant attendants demand that you pay – usually 1zł or 2zł (although this habit is gradually dying out).

Women's toilets are marked with a circle, men's with a triangle.

Tour operators

Kirker Holidays (tel: 020 7593 1899; www.kirkerholidays.com) offer short breaks to Krakow, while Baltic Holidays (tel: 0845 070 5711 in UK; 401 429 6614 from the US; www.balticholidays.com) offers packages as well as tailor-made trips, as does Regent Holidays (tel: 020 7666 1244; www.regentholidays.co.uk) a long-time specialist in Eastern Europe.

Postcards for sale

Tourist information

In Krakow

The official **Krakow City Tourist Office** has several InfoKraków branches throughout the city:

Cloth Hall, Main Market Square 1–3 (tel: 012 433 73 10; daily 9am–7pm, until 5pm winter)

Wyspiański Pavillion 2000, pl. Wszystkich Świętych 2 (tel: 012 616 18 86; daily 9am–5pm)

ul. Szpitalna 25 (tel: 012 432 01 10; daily 9am–7pm, until 5pm winter)

Kraków International Airport – Balice (tel: 012 285 53 41; daily 9.30am–7.30pm)

ul. św. Jana 2 (tel: 012 421 77 87; daily 10am–6pm)

ul. Józefa, Kazimierz (tel: 012 422 04 71; daily 9am–5pm).

The Tourist Information Call Centre is open daily 9am–7pm (tel: 012 432 00 60).

Other information centres include:

Małopolska Region Tourist Information Office (ul. Grodzka 31; tel: 012 421 77 06; www.mcit.pl; May–Oct Mon–Fri 9am–8pm, Sat–Sun 9am–4pm, Nov–Apr Mon–Fri 9am–5pm, Sat–Sun 10am–2pm).

The **Jewish Cultural Information Office** (Centrum Kultury Żydowskiej, ul. Meiselsa 17, Kazimierz; tel: 012 430 64 49; www.judaica.pl; Mon–Fri 10am–8pm, Sat–Sun 10am–2pm) has information on Jewish cultural events.

Zakopane Tourist Information Centre (ul. Kosciuski 17; tel: 018 201 22 11; www.zakopane.pl; Mon–Fri 9am–5pm). Sells good hiking maps as well as a decent guide to the resort's ski-run network and lift-ticket system.

Outside of Poland

UK: Polish National Tourist Office, Westgate House, West Gate, London W5 1YY; tel: 0300 303 1812; www.poland.travel.

US: Polish National Tourist Office, 5 Marine View Plaza, Hoboken, New Jersey, NJ 07030; tel: 201 420 99 10; www.poland.travel.

Transport

Arrival

By air: Krakow's John Paul II International Airport at Balice is the second-busiest airport in Poland, and currently resembles a building site as it undergoes major reconstruction until late 2015. It is served by direct flights to and from many European cities throughout the year. Flight time from London is just over two hours. Seasonal direct flights operate from cities such as Chicago and New York.

By rail: There are various train routes between London and Krakow, involving as many as six or as few as two changes. One of the quickest involves changing in Paris and then Berlin and takes a little less than 24 hours; though the route via Brussels, Cologne and Frankfurt is faster it involves more

You can take a bus to Zakopane   *Tourist information*

changes. Both Voyages-SNCF (tel: 0844 848 58 48; uk.voyages-sncf.com) and Deutsche Bahn (tel: 08718 80 80 66; www.bahn.com) book train journeys across Europe.

There are also regular train services between Krakow and other main Polish cities. Express trains between Krakow and Warsaw, which need to be booked in advance, take about 2 hours 45 minutes. For information and booking contact Polish State Railways (Polskie Koleje Państwowe; tel: 19 757 or 022 39 19757 from outside Poland; www.pkp.pl).

Neither PKP telephone lines nor train station information desks have many English speakers, though staff will try to find someone to help you, but the colour-coded timetables are easy to follow: yellow for departures (*odjazdy*); white for arrivals (*przyjazdy*).

Express trains usually feature the prefix 'ex', and direct trains are indicated as *pospieszny*. Trains marked *osobowy* are slow, sometimes very slow.

The main railway station is within easy walking distance of the historic centre, though the traffic system obliges taxis leaving the terminus to take a slightly more circuitous route to the centre.

By road: Coach travel is very cheap in Poland. In Krakow, regional and international coaches leave from the coach station (Malopolskie Dworzec Autobusowy; tel: 0703 40 33 40 for bookings and information; www.mda.malopolska.pl) in ul. Bosacka next to the rail-way station. One of the best-connected private services is Eurolines Polska (tel: 032 351 20 20; www.eurolines-polska.pl). The journey from Krakow to Warsaw can be long because coaches often stop at a number of cities en route.

Airport

Krakow's John Paul II International Airport (ul. Kapitana Medweckiego 1; tel: 012 295 58 00, 080 105 50 00; www.krakowairport.pl), 18km (11 miles) east of the city in Balice, is currently the subject of a massive reconstruction plan that will increase it to three times the size and modernise the train station. All the while the airport remains open with the basic operation unaffected (see its website for up-to-date information).

Getting to the city: The best option is by train, although the train service has been suspended until sometime in 2015, while the station is renovated. As such, bus is presently the best way to get to and from the airport. Public buses 292 (every 20 minutes) and 208 (once an hour) both make the journey; turn right out of the international terminal to find the bus stop. Alternatively, outside the terminal you'll find plenty of official PT taxis (tel: 012 191 91) waiting. Make sure the meter is running and expect to pay no more than 70zł.

Transport within Krakow

Public transport in Krakow is both cheap and reliable. The fabulous tram sys-

Trains will take you out of town

tem provides the perfect way of getting around, from 5am to 11pm. Tram tickets cost 2.80zł a ride on one tram over any distance. Better value are 24-hour (15zł), 48-hour (24zł) and 72-hour (36zł) tickets. Buy them from most kiosks, or anywhere you see a 'Sprzeda Biletów mpk' sign.

Tickets must be validated in one of the yellow machines when boarding. Watch a local do it first if you're unsure.

Be careful when getting off trams in the city centre, where they share the roads with cars: you're essentially stepping down into traffic, and drivers do not always give tram passengers priority.

For bus and tram information, tel: 19150; www.mpk.krakow.pl.

Trains: The newly modernised main railway station, just a short walk from the historic centre, is Krakow Główny (Dworzec Główny, pl. Jeziorańksiego 3, tel: 19 757 or 22 194 36). You can catch a train from here to Oświęcim for the Auschwitz-Birkenau concentration camp and to Krakow Płaszów for connections to the Wieliczka salt mine.

Taxis: Although the town centre is essentially pedestrianised, taxis do have access. There are cab ranks around Main Market Square, although it is not very practical or necessary to use taxis to get around the centre. Radio taxis, which can be booked by phone, are generally cheaper than taxis from ranks, though the latter are not very expensive.

For longer journeys, negotiate the fare with the driver before departure. Some reliable cab companies are:

Euro Taxi, tel: 012 96 64

Mega Taxi, tel: 012 96 25

Radio Taxi, tel: 012 91 91

Expect to pay a 7.50zł starting rate plus 2.30–7zł per kilometre depending on time of day.

Car rental: Krakow's compact size generally makes hiring a car more trouble than it's worth. However, for visiting other destinations, a car can be a good idea.

Arrangements and conditions for car hire are similar to those in other countries. The minimum age requirement is 21 and you must have been in possession of a valid licence for at least one year. US and Canadian licences are accepted, as are international driving licences. Ask if collision damage waiver insurance is included in the price.

Avis: ul. Lubicz 23; tel: 012 629 61 08; www.avis.pl (also at the airport).

Budget: Ul. Medweckiego 1 (airport); tel: 012 285 50 25; www.budget.pl.

Cracowrent: ul. Kamieńskiego 41; tel: 012 265 26 50; www.cracowrent.pl.

Europcar: ul. Nadwiślańska 6 (at the Qubus Hotel); tel: 012 374 56 96; www.europcar.com.pl.

Hertz: al. Focha 1 (inside the Cracovia Hotel); tel: 012 429 62 62; www.hertz.com.pl.

Joka: ul. Zacisze 7; tel: 012 429 66 30; www.joka.com.pl.

The town's main train station

National: ul. Głowackiego 22 (inside the Demel hotel); tel: 505 761 461; www.nationalcar.com.pl.

Driving: It's a sobering fact that Polish traffic fatality figures are among the worst in Europe, a testament to the appalling condition of the roads and the often-unsafe driving practices of the locals.

For those who insist on driving in Krakow, be warned that road works are everywhere. If you find yourself following a tram on a stretch of road that doesn't have a separate, fenced-off area for them, proceed with caution. You are expected to stop when trams do, regardless of what lane you're in, as people will be getting on and off, and will be doing so via the road you are driving down.

You can drive in Poland on an EU or US licence. Dipped headlights must be switched on at all times year-round; seat belts are compulsory front and back and the maximum blood-alcohol limit is 0.02 percent.

Poles drive on the right-hand side of the road.

Speed limits are 140km/h (87mph) on motorways, 120km/h (75mph) on dual carriageways, 100km/h (62mph) on single carriageways, 90km/h (56mph) outside urban areas, and 50km/h (31mph) in built-up areas during the daytime and 60km/h (37mph) at night. You may be fined on the spot for speeding.

Parking: Because of the frequency of car theft and break-ins in and around the city, it's advisable to use guarded car parks. There are only two car parks in the centre, at Plac św. Ducha and Plac Szcepański. Neither is very large, and both are very popular.

Additional car parks within walking distance of the centre include by the main railway and bus stations, pl. Biskupi, ul. Zyblikiewicza, ul. Lubicz, Galleria Królewska, and ul. Powiśle by Wawel Castle.

Petrol (gas): Petrol stations are common on major roads; most stay open around the clock and all sell the full range of petrol, diesel and lpg.

V

Visas and passports

Holders of European Union passports do not need a visa to enter Poland and may stay as long as they please. Visitors holding passports from many other countries may also enter Poland without a visa, but their stay may be limited, usually for 90 days.

Poland is a member of the Schengen group of countries, meaning that a Schengen Block visa is valid for entry to Poland.

Travellers may need to fulfil additional medical, insurance and financial requirements to be granted a visa. Visa applications need to be registered online at www.e-konsulat.gov.pl, where there is more detailed visa information. Minimum visa processing times range from 10 days to a month, depending on the passport held, and can take longer.

Trilingual exit sign

LANGUAGE

Polish, a Slavic language, has a complex grammar and can be difficult to pronounce with its long sequences of consonants. As a general rule, the accent falls on the penultimate syllable. The majority of tourist industry staff in Krakow speak good English and/or German, and efforts have been made in recent years to translate signs and menus for English-speaking visitors. Attempting a few basic words is likely to be appreciated by the locals, however. Here are some key words and phrases to get you started.

General

Yes *Tak*
No *Nie*
Please *Proszę*
Thank you *Dziękuję*
Excuse me *Przepraszam*
You're welcome *Proszę*
Hello/Hi *Dzień dobry/Cześć* **(informal)**
Goodbye *Dowidzenia/Cześć* **(informal)**
Do you speak English? *Czy mówisz po angielsku?*
I don't understand *Nie rozumiem*
I'm sorry *Przepraszam*
I don't know *Nie wiem*
My name is... *Mam na imię...*
Nice to meet you *Miło poznać*
What is your name? *Jak masz na imię?*
I am English/American *Jestem z Anglii/ z Ameryki*
When? *Kiedy?*
At what time? *O której?*

today *dzisiaj*
yesterday *wczoraj*
tomorrow *jutro*
now/later *teraz/później*
morning *rano*
afternoon *popołudnie*
evening *wieczór*
day/week *dzień/tydzień*
month/year *miesiąc/rok*
left *lewo*
right *prawo*

On arrival

Where is there a bus/tram stop? *Gdzie jest przystanek autobusowy/tramwajowy?*
railway station *dworzec kolejowy*
airport *lotnisko*
cab rank *postój taksówek*
one-way ticket *bilet w jedną stronę*
return ticket *bilet w dwie strony*
I'd like a single/double room *Poproszę pokój jednoosobowy/dwuosobowy*
What is the charge per night? *Ile kosztuje doba?*

Emergencies

Help! *Pomocy!*
Call a doctor/an ambulance *Proszę wezwać lekarza/karetkę*
Call the police/fire brigade *Proszę wezwać policję/straż pożarną*
Where's the nearest hospital? *Gdzie jest najbliższy szpital?*
I am sick *Jestem chory(a)*

Hairdresser sign

I have lost my money/passport/luggage *Zgubiłem(am) pieniądze/passport/bagaż*
pharmacy/chemists *apteka*

Shopping

How much is it? *Ile to kosztuje?*
Have you got…? *Czy ma Pani/Pan…?*
enough *wystarczy*
too much *za dużo*
a piece *kawałek*
each *każdy*
Do you take credit cards? *Czy można płacić kartą?*
Is there a bank/ATM near here? *Czy jest w pobliżu bank/bankomat?*
shopping centre (mall) *centrum handlowe*
market *rynek*
supermarket *supermarket*
open *otwarte*
closed *zamknięte*

Sightseeing

Where is…? *Gdzie jest…?*
tourist information office *informacja turystyczna*
church *kościół*
exhibition *wystawa*
museum *museum*
guide *przewodnik*
free *za darmo*

Dining out

breakfast *śniadanie*
lunch *lunch/obiad*
dinner *kolacja*
meal *posiłek*

first course *pierwsze danie*
main course *drugie danie*
the bill *rachunek*
I am a vegetarian *Jestem wegetarianinem/wegetarianką*
I'd like to order *Chciał(a)bym zamówić*
Enjoy your meal! *Smacznego!*
tip *napiwek*
smoking *dla palących*
non-smoking *dla niepalących*

Days of the week

Monday *poniedziałek*
Tuesday *wtorek*
Wednesday *środa*
Thursday *czwartek*
Friday *piątek*
Saturday *sobota*
Sunday *niedziela*

Numbers

0 *zero*
1 *jeden*
2 *dwa*
3 *trzy*
4 *cztery*
5 *pięć*
6 *sześć*
7 *siedem*
8 *osiem*
9 *dziewięć*
10 *dziesięć*
20 *dwadzieścia*
30 *trzydzieści*
40 *czterdzieści*
50 *pięćdziesiąt*
100 *sto*
1000 *tysiąc*

Wisława Szymborska

BOOKS AND FILM

Poland has a long, proud literary tradition that stretches back to medieval times, when scribes such as Jan Długosz (1415–80) chronicled the events of the era. In the following centuries, Polish talents including the Romantic poet Adam Mickiewicz (1798–1855) and the Nobel Prize-winning author Henryk Sienkiewicz (1846–1916) came to the fore, blending Romanticism with patriotism during a time of Tsarist hegemony. As Poland's self-declared cultural capital, Krakow was awarded Unesco's City of Literature in 2013.

When it comes to film, the city is home to April's week-long Krakow International Film Festival, one of the most respected film festivals in the country, as well as the oldest. Although the city may not be Poland's answer to Hollywood (that title goes to Łódź), cinephiles will be intrigued by Krakow's real and filmic history. In particular, the impact of Steven Spielberg's Oscar-winning *Schindler's List*, which was based and shot in Krakow, has been key to the city's international profile. The city offers many cinemas, including one with allegedly the biggest screen in Europe.

Books

Fiction

Solaris, by Stanisław Lem (1921–2006). Science-fiction writer and former Jagiellonian University medical student stands out as one of Poland's best-known authors, with his seminal work twice turned into film.

The Captive Mind, by Czesław Miłosz (1911–2004). Miłosz is popularly considered as Poland's finest writer of the 20th century, and his 1953 defining masterpiece, is a fascinating study of the human psyche. Miłosz was awarded the Nobel Prize for Literature in 1980 and spent much of his time in Kraków both before and after the fall of the Iron Curtain.

The Madman and the Nun and *The Crazy Locomotive*, by Stanisław Ignacy Witkiewicz (1885–1939). Also known as Witkacy, he was one of the great avant-garde figures of inter-war Poland. Heavily influenced by drugs and depression, his works include plays, paintings and novels.

Holocaust

Schindler's Ark, by Thomas Keneally (b.1935). This novel, set in Schindler's Podgórze factory and the nearby Płaszów labour camp, paints a vivid picture of wartime Krakow.

If this is a Man, by Primo Levi (1919–87). Levi, an Italian chemist and Holocaust survivor, tells his story, with detached prose picking up the minutiae and describing in detail the dehumanisation process experienced by inmates.

Schindler's List

Chilling Auschwitz sign

This Way for the Gas, Ladies and Gentlemen, by Tadeusz Borowski (1922–51). Borowski describes his incarceration in Auschwitz. A chilling story of daily survival.

Auschwitz, by Sybille Steinbacher (b.1966). This recent book provides a fine historical overview.

Poetry

Kraków-based Wisława Szymborska (1923–2012) is regarded one of Poland's greatest poets. Despite penning fewer than 250 poems, she was a well-known figure who won international recognition when awarded the Nobel Prize for Literature in 1996.

Film

Schindler's List

Based on Thomas Keneally's 1982 book **Schindler's Ark**, Steven Spielberg's 1993 film **Schindler's List** tells the true story of Nazi Party member and businessman Oskar Schindler (1908–74; see page 83), who moved to Krakow shortly after the German invasion in 1939 and opened a factory in Podgórze. The factory was staffed by Jewish employees, whom Schindler did his best to protect, with the film following the story through to the final liquidation of Krakow's Jews and Schindler's mostly successful attempts to save his staff with the aid of the list of the film's title. Schindler fled after the war, taking refuge as a farmer in Argentina before finally returning to Germany, where he died. His factory survived and is one of the many Jewish pilgrimage sites around the city. Ralph Fiennes' portrayal of SS camp commandant Amon Göth is a tour de force.

Polish film

The Double Life of Veronique (1991). A joint Polish-French drama film with scenes shot in Krakow.

Our God's Brother (1997). The story of a young priest, a film made from the play written by Pope John Paul II.

The Pianist (2002). Roman Polański's Oscar-winning film of the true story of a Polish-Jewish pianist's life in World War II Warsaw.

Karol: A Man Who Became Pope (2005). A biography of Karol Wojtyła who was Bishop of Krakow and went on to be Pope John Paul II.

Pope John Paul II (2005). A TV mini-series on the Pope's life.

Inland Empire (2006). David Lynch's bizarre mystery film was shot mainly in Łódź.

Katyń (2007) tells the story behind the infamous Katyń Massacre in which the KGB murdered 20,000 Polish officers in 1940.

33 Scenes from Life (2008). This is a charismatic film about human loss, which was acclaimed by international film critics.

Walesa. Man of Hope (2013). The story of Nobel Peace Prize winner Lech Walesa and his Solidarity Movement.

ABOUT THIS BOOK

This *Explore Guide* has been produced by the editors of Insight Guides, whose books have set the standard for visual travel guides since 1970. With top-quality photography and authoritative recommendations, these guidebooks bring you the very best routes and itineraries in the world's most exciting destinations.

BEST ROUTES

The routes in the book provide something to suit all budgets, tastes and trip lengths. As well as covering the destination's many classic attractions, the itineraries track lesser-known sights, and there are also excursions for those who want to extend their visit outside the city. The routes embrace a range of interests, so whether you are an art fan, a gourmet, a history buff or have kids to entertain, you will find an option to suit.

We recommend reading the whole of a route before setting out. This should help you to familiarise yourself with it and enable you to plan where to stop for refreshments – options are shown in the 'Food and Drink' box at the end of each tour.

For our pick of the tours by theme, consult Recommended Routes for... (see pages 4–5).

INTRODUCTION

The routes are set in context by this introductory section, giving an overview of the destination to set the scene, plus background information on food and drink, shopping and more, while a succinct history timeline highlights the key events over the centuries.

DIRECTORY

Also supporting the routes is a Directory chapter, with a clearly organised A–Z of practical information, our pick of where to stay while you are there and select restaurant listings; these eateries complement the more low-key cafés and restaurants that feature within the routes and are intended to offer a wider choice for evening dining. Also included here are some nightlife listings, plus a handy language guide and our recommendations for books and films about the destination.

ABOUT THE AUTHORS

Craig Turp has written a number of books on the languages and peoples of Central and Eastern Europe. Many of the tours were originally conceived by Poland specialist Ian Wisniewski. Renata Rubnikowicz first visited Poland as a child, and her first of many trips to Krakow was in the 1980s during the days of Solidarity, when the city was very different to the one visitors enjoy today. Thanks also go to Jackie Staddon and Hilary Weston.

CONTACT THE EDITORS

We hope you find this Explore Guide useful, interesting and a pleasure to read. If you have any questions or feedback on the text, pictures or maps, please do let us know. If you have noticed any errors or outdated facts, or have suggestions for places to include on the routes, we would be delighted to hear from you. Please drop us an email at insight@apaguide.co.uk. Thanks!

CREDITS

Explore Krakow

Contributors: Craig Turp, Ian Wisniewski, Renata Rubnikowicz, Jackie Staddon, Hilary Weston
Commissioning Editor: Carine Tracanelli
Series Editor: Sarah Clark
Pictures/Art: Tom Smyth/Shahid Mahmood
Map Production: original cartography Berndtson & Berndtson, updated by Apa Cartography Department
Production: Tynan Dean and Rebeka Davies

Photo credits: Alamy 4MC, 30, 31R, 41R, 40/41, 58, 70, 74, 136/137; PA Images 136; Corrie Wingate/Apa Publications 2ML, 2MC, 2MR, 2MR, 2MC, 2ML, 5MR, 5MR, 6ML, 6ML, 6MC, 6MR, 8/9, 10, 11R, 14/15, 18, 19, 22ML, 22MC, 22MR, 22ML, 22MC, 22MR, 22/23T, 25, 26, 28, 28/29, 29R, 30/31, 32, 33R, 32/33, 34, 34/35, 46, 48, 48/49, 49R, 50, 50/51, 51R, 52, 53, 54, 56/57, 57R, 58/59, 60, 61R, 62/63, 63R, 65, 66, 67R, 68, 69, 70/71, 71R, 72, 72/73, 73R, 75R, 76, 79R, 80, 81R, 80/81, 82, 83R, 84, 85R, 84/85, 86, 87R, 86/87, 88, 89, 90, 90/91, 91R, 92, 93, 94, 95, 96, 97R, 96/97, 98, 99R, 98/99, 100ML, 100MR, 100MR, 100MC, 100ML, 113, 120, 121T, 121B, 124/125, 126, 127, 128, 129R, 128/129, 130, 130/131, 131R, 132, 133, 134, 135, 137R; Dreamstime 1, 2/3T, 6/7T, 8, 9R, 10/11, 12, 13, 24, 35R, 36/37, 60/61, 62, 77, 82/83, 110/111, 114, 124, 125R; Getty Images 21; Gregory Wrona/Apa Publications 4TL, 4ML, 4BC, 5T, 5M, 6MC, 6MR, 14, 15R, 16, 16/17, 17R, 38, 39, 40, 42, 43, 44, 44/45, 45R, 47R, 46/47, 54/55, 55R, 56, 59R, 64, 74/75, 78, 100MC, 100/101T, 102, 103, 104, 105, 106, 107, 112, 115, 116, 117, 118, 119, 122, 123; iStock 78/79, 108/109; Mary Evans Picture Library 20; Robert Harding 27, 66/67
Cover credits: Wawel Cathedral, *4Corners Images* **Front Cover BL:** dolls *Corrie Wingate/Apa* **Back Cover: (Left)** Main Square *Dreamstime* **(Right):** St. Mary's Basilica, *Dreamstime*

Printed by CTPS – China
© 2014 Apa Publications (UK) Ltd
All Rights Reserved

First Edition 2014

DISTRIBUTION

Worldwide
APA Publications GmbH & Co. Verlag KG (Singapore branch)
7030 Ang Mo Kio Ave 5, 08-65
Northstar @ AMK, Singapore 569880
Email: apasin@singnet.com.sg
UK and Ireland
Dorling Kindersley Ltd (a Penguin Company)
80 Strand, London, WC2R 0RL, UK
Email: sales@uk.dk.com
US
Ingram Publisher Services
One Ingram Blvd, PO Box 3006, La Vergne, TN 37086-1986
Email: ips@ingramcontent.com
Australia and New Zealand
Woodslane
10 Apollo St, Warriewood NSW 2102, Australia
Email: info@woodslane.com.au

INDEX

MAP LEGEND

● Start of tour

→ Tour & route direction

❶ Recommended sight

❷ Recommended restaurant/café

★ Place of interest

ⓘ Tourist information

🛈 Statue/monument

✉ Main post office

🚌 Main bus station

✺ Viewpoint

Park

Important building

Hotel

Transport hub

Market/store

Pedestrian area

Urban area

INSIGHT GUIDES

INSPIRING YOUR NEXT ADVENTURE

Insight Guides offers you a range of travel guides
to match your needs. Whether you are looking for
inspiration for planning a trip, cultural information,
walks and tours, great listings, or practical advice, we
have a product to suit you.

www.insightguides.com